THIS DANGEROUS MENACE

THIS DANGEROUS MENACE

DUNDEE AND THE RIVER TAY AT WAR, 1939 TO 1945

by ANDREW JEFFREY

MAINSTREAM
PUBLISHING

EDINBURGH AND LONDON

The moral right of the author has been asserted
First published in Great Britain 1991 by
MAINSTREAM PUBLISHING COMPANY (EDINBURGH) LTD
7 Albany Street
Edinburgh EH1 3UG

ISBN 1 85158 492 7

A catalogue record for this book is available from the British Library

Typeset in 11/13pt Garamond by Blackpool Typesetting Services Ltd, Blackpool
Printed and bound in Great Britain by
Butler & Tanner Ltd, Frome and London

Dundee, 12 March 1941.

'. . . I would ask you, if you can, not to worry as I am guided by a bright star which has always brought me home safely.

You must have faith, as we do here amongst magnificent people who never weaken and who constantly provide an excellent example to those around them. We who have abandoned everything; family, home, livelihood, for a life of constant struggle in self-imposed exile, and who may one day give up even more, to us that example is one of simple courage and belief in the common cause.

Whatever happens, you must keep your spirits up; we have always steered the correct course and will continue to do so without fear . . .'

Extract from a letter sent by Capitaine de Corvette Georges Cabanier,
Captain of the Free French submarine Rubis *based in Dundee,*
to his wife Jacqueline, then in Casablanca.

Contents

Preface

In the late 1930s Dundee was a city in the grip of a fundamental and deepening crisis.

As a result of the development of cheaper substitutes, foreign competition and the rapid increase in the bulk handling of cargoes, the city's staple jute industry was in terminal decline. The Chamber of Commerce was voicing its fears to the Board of Trade and warning of an imminent trade war with India.

Employment in the city's jute mills had plummeted from 35,000 to 20,000 in the decade between 1928 and 1938 and, with 14,000 unemployed, there was an urgent need to attract new industries to the area. This decline in the economic base of the city was further exacerbated by the worldwide depression of the Thirties, the effects of which were to linger in Dundee longer than in the rest of the country, causing unemployment to remain stubbornly high well into the war.

The city's unemployment problems were aggravated by the practice of the jute barons of almost exclusively employing poorly paid female labour. Male labour was used, but largely in the form of boys employed as 'loom doffers' who were promptly sacked when they reached 18 and qualified for full wages. This ensured the continued existence of a large reservoir of unskilled male unemployed for whom the only answer was to leave, often by way of the forces recruitment offices. One result of this exodus was the creation of a serious imbalance in the city's population; a survey quoted in *The Times* in 1943 showed that there were 15,000 more women on the voters roll than men. Not surprisingly Dundee was known as a woman's town.

The growth of the jute industry had been rapid following the arrival of the first cargo in April 1840; within 20 years the population had grown from 60,000 to 100,000 and by 1911 had reached 165,000. By the Thirties this uncontrolled growth had resulted in seemingly intractable social problems; housing conditions were, even by the standards of the time, simply appalling.

Infant mortality was frighteningly high and getting worse, disease was rife and adult life expectancy low.

This, then, was the shape of a city which found itself being dragged into the vortex of a world war for the second time in 25 years.

In the years since 1945, largely due to the fact that the city escaped serious air attack by the Luftwaffe, the belief has become widespread that, apart from sending 12,000 of its men and women off to the fighting services, Dundee did not play a significant part in the war. The aim of this book is to disprove that theory. Further, it is widely believed that the war years were a period when people, inspired by dynamic leadership, pulled together in the face of adversity. Nostalgia, however, is not conducive of objectivity and it is hardly surprising to find that the reality of wartime was a long way removed from the 'beer and skittles' myth.

Despite being concerned with a mere six years in the history of the city and the surrounding area, this book can lay no claim to being definitive. Of necessity it is episodic, seeking only to give a picture of life in and around the city from 1938 to 1945.

The first brush with Hitler came with the arrest of Jessie Jordan, a German spy who operated from that unlikely hotbed of international intrigue – the Hilltown. No sooner had that story left the front pages than it was followed by the slow and depressingly chaotic development of Civil Defence, Munich, the inexorable slide into war and the military build up in the area which followed the defeats in Norway, the Low Countries and France.

Enemy action against the east coast began in the early weeks of the war and reached a peak in the period between November 1940 and May 1941, finally fading away with the German invasion of Russia in June that year. Offensive action by British and allied forces based in and around Dundee started within hours of the commencement of hostilities and continued right up to the very end of the war in Europe in May 1945.

As the war began to draw to its inevitable conclusion, the city began to look anew at its future and to restarting the regeneration, abruptly halted in 1939, after only the first hesitant steps had been taken.

To the many who have contributed to this book, my thanks; to those whose deeds and dedication have gone unremarked, my apologies. Every effort has been made to ensure accuracy and should there be errors of fact or substance, they are mine alone.

ANDREW JEFFREY, *Dundee, 1991*

Chapter One

Jessie Jordan – The Other Dundee Courier

Shortly before 11.00 am on Wednesday, 2 March 1938, two police cars drew up outside a hairdresser's shop at the corner of Rosebank Street and Kinloch Street in Dundee. Earlier, a plain-clothes policewoman had ensured that the owner, a blonde woman in her early fifties, was at work. Her visitors were Chief Constable Joseph Neilans of Dundee Police, two of his officers, Detective Lieutenant John Carstairs and Policewoman Annie Ross, and Lieutenant Colonel Edward Hinchley-Cooke, Assistant Director of MI5. A crowd was soon attracted by the police cars, though at first there was little to see other than the cards in the window advertising 'Vienna Perms' and 'J. Jordan, Hair Specialist'.

At midday Jessie Jordan was arrested and charged with offences under the Official Secrets Acts. She was a German spy.

Jessie Wallace was born in Glasgow in April 1887, the illegitimate daughter of a housemaid from Partick. As her mother was in service in Coatbridge, Jessie spent her early years with her grandmother until, when she was four, her mother married a railwayman from Perth and took her to live there.

Her childhood was beset with problems; she was unwanted, she had to bear the considerable stigma in Victorian times of illegitimacy and, by her own account, her home life was characterised by the brutality of both her mother and stepfather.

At the Western District School she showed little academic promise but displayed considerable ability as a needleworker and dressmaker. She was to remain intensely proud of having had some of her work exhibited at the 1901 Empire Exhibition in Glasgow.

She left home at 16, taking her first job as a maid in a house on Kinnoull Hill. Soon, however, her restless nature took her to other jobs in the Isle of Man, Liverpool and Manchester, none of which she kept for long. In 1907, aged 20 and unemployed, she came to visit her mother who was by then living in Dundee.

Jessie Jordan.
DUNDEE COURIER AND EVENING TELEGRAPH

That September an 18-year-old German, Fritz Jordan, started work as a waiter at the Royal Hotel in Union Street, Dundee. Fritz had come to Britain with his brother, Hans, to look for work. He had been at the hotel for only two days when news came that Hans had been killed in an accident at work in London. Years later Jessie described how she first met Fritz on the stairs of the hotel, holding the telegram from London and visibly upset. He had only limited English and came to rely heavily on Jessie in the ensuing weeks. A romance blossomed and they were married in August 1912 in Fritz's home town of Hannover. In May 1914 Jessie gave birth to a daughter, Margaretha Frieda Wilhelmina. As a loyal German couple they chose the last name in honour of Kaiser Wilhelm, then riding high on a heady mixture of popularity and fervent nationalism.

Fritz was called up for military service in August 1914, and in 1916 Jessie, restless as ever, moved to Hamburg where she started in business as a beautician. Two years later the war was going badly for Germany and life became increasingly difficult for someone who, although a German citizen by marriage, was nevertheless British-born.

Having survived four years in the trenches, Fritz died from pneumonia at the very end of the war. In 1919, as a result of both her personal difficulties and the death of her husband, Jessie was to be found back at her mother's home in Perth. Again she was unable to settle and soon returned to Hamburg where, the following year, she married her landlord, a German Jew called Baumgarten. This marriage was a failure and, following the divorce, Jessie reverted to the name Jordan.

During the Twenties and early Thirties Jessie channelled her considerable energies into a successful hairdressing business in Hamburg which eventually extended to three shops in fashionable suburbs of the city. In 1932 her daughter Marga had married Herman Wobrock, an agent for hairdressing equipment and, two years later, had given birth to a girl they christened Jessie. Having a fine soprano voice, Marga was also developing a career as a singer when the mixture of bad luck and bad judgment, which would bedevil both her life and that of her mother, intervened.

By 1936 the Nazis had consolidated their grip on power in Germany and Marga found that her career was effectively at an end unless she could prove that she was of racially pure descent. Bearing in mind that her mother was illegitimate, this was not going to be easy. In addition, an affair with a Greek hypnotist led to the swift break up of her marriage.

Earlier, Jessie had acted as guarantor of loans taken out to finance the expansion of Herman Wobrock's business. This had failed, with the result that Jessie was forced to liquidate her own business to meet the debts. However, prior to this, Jessie's status as a successful businesswoman had brought her into the social circle inhabited by the local Nazi hierarchy. Despite her having been married to a Jew, her naivety and a desire to climb the social ladder led her to cultivate these associations.

Throughout her life in Germany, Jessie had maintained only patchy contact with her family in Scotland, but with her business sold and Marga's marriage and career wrecked, she must have welcomed a letter from her stepbrother, William Haddow, in December 1936. An engine driver from Perth, he wrote to say that his wife Mary had died and that he needed a housekeeper for his two children. Jessie decided to return to Scotland, take up her stepbrother's offer and, with the help of her family, attempt to prove Marga's Aryan background, thus rescuing her career.

News of her decision soon reached a Nazi party official and talent spotter for the German Secret Service, and she was targeted for recruitment as an agent.

When Hitler came to power in 1933, steps were taken to develop the Abwehr, or German Secret Service, as an effective instrument of Nazi policy. Athough in the early days this was to lead to a number of rather hasty innovations and an element of trusting to luck, within three years major successes were being achieved. From its Berlin headquarters, Abwehr established a series of strategically located out-stations, the largest of which, Abwehrstelle X, was set up in a grey concrete building near the end of Sophienstrasse, in the Harvesthude district of Hamburg.

American money and manpower had effectively sealed Germany's fate at the end of the First World War and the new Nazi government was eager for an assessment of the threat America posed to its expansionist plans in Europe. Maintaining excellent maritime links with both Britain and America, Hamburg was ideally placed for the task given to Abwehr station chief, Captain Herbert Wichmann – spying on both these countries.

One of Wichmann's early recruits in America was a doctor of German extraction, Ignatz Theodor Griebl. A Lieutenant in the US Army Medical Reserve and a notorious womaniser, Griebl was acknowledged as leader of the German community in Yorkville, Manhattan. In 1934, through his brother's friendship with Joseph Goebbels, he offered his services as a spy for Germany. Abwehr accepted the offer and made the senior naval intelligence officer, Hamburg, Captain Erich Pfieffer, case officer.

A substantial spy ring was set up and run by Griebl from amongst the large German community in New York which began passing a variety of high grade, largely technical, intelligence back to Germany. The spy ring had essentially two roles; first, the acquisition of technical and industrial information, especially in the armaments industry, and second, obtaining information about defences. Linked closely with the Griebl ring was one run from Germany by Lieutenant Commander Herman Menzel which used the overseas representatives of companies such as Krupps in industrial espionage. Another ring, controlled by Hamburg's head of air intelligence, Major Nikolaus Ritter, pulled off Abwehr's greatest pre-war coup – the stealing of the plans of the new Norden bombsight. It is known that, amongst many other things, the Griebl ring was able to pass over detailed specifications of pursuit aircraft being built at the Seversky plant on Long Island and the Sperry gyroscope, along with blueprints of three new destroyers and a new Navy scout bomber, and various codes, maps and models. Some of this information was later traded with Japan.

The effectiveness of a spy is measured, not by the amount of information he or she gathers, but by the amount which reaches his or her employers, and it is here that spies are most vulnerable to detection. Radio remains the easiest and fastest means of transmission but, in the days before computer-scrambled burst transmission, it was the least secure. In the mid-1930s Germany was leading the way in the development of micro-photography. The equipment, however, was still bulky and impractical. Most of the information collected by German spies active at this time was sent in the form of copies of original documents, photographs and reports. The system run from Hamburg used an elaborate combination of the public mailing system and a network of cut-outs, or breaks in the chain of communication, and couriers. It was designed to avoid at all costs the sending of material directly to Germany as it was at least likely that such mail would be opened by the security services. One of the couriers was Johanna Hoffman, a hairdresser who worked on the German transatlantic liner *Europa*. Another was Jessie Jordan.

Jessie had been booked on a sailing from Hamburg to Leith on 2 February 1937, but was deceived into missing her boat. Later that day, she was persuaded to work for Abwehr.

Of the factors which motivate spies, by far the rarest is patriotism or political conviction. Much more common is the lure of easy money. Whilst she had a practised eye for the finer things in life, by her own admission Jessie's motivation was the most common of all; a craving for excitement and, above all, enhanced self-esteem. After her arrest it was said that Jessie had felt threatened by the anti-Jewish pogroms in Germany. The facts do not support this. If that were the case, and particularly as she was British-born, she and Marga could simply have joined the flood of refugees leaving the country at the time. Most of her activities for Abwehr were undertaken when the whole family were resident in Scotland, and someone in fear of her life would hardly have made such frequent trips back to Germany. In addition, on a number of occasions while she was in Scotland, she expressed some sympathy for Nazism.

After eight days of intensive briefing Jessie finally sailed, reaching William Haddow's home at 16 Breadalbane Terrace in Perth on 16 February. It was to be some weeks before she summoned up the courage to undertake her first assignment for Abwehr, which was to secure information on the Royal Naval Armaments Depot at Crombie, near Rosyth. Taking a train to Dunfermline and a bus to Charleston, she then walked to a short stretch of road overlooking the depot from where, unobserved, she drew a plan of the installations and the surrounding area.

In mid-June Jessie took one of her nephews to visit her aunt at Brecon in Wales and there discussed the possibility of starting a new hairdressing business for which her aunt would put up the capital. Thus provided with excellent cover, and leaving her nephew in Brecon, she set off for Southampton, saying she was going to look for a shop. There, under the pretext of seeing an acquaintance off on a ship to South Africa, she took a number of photographs of the docks and other installations. Encouraged by her success to date, she took a train from Southampton to Aldershot where she walked right into the barracks and began noting down information.

On a subsequent visit to Edinburgh she bought a map of the east coast and, using the excuse of taking the Haddow children on trips to the seaside, she began noting on it various coastal defence works and installations such as coastguard stations. While she was on just such a trip to Carnoustie, on Tuesday, 27 July 1937, an advert in the *Dundee Courier* caught her eye.

> Ladies and Gents Hairdressing Saloons, Stationer and Tobacconist (combined) for sale. Cheap for quick disposal. 36 Advertiser.

Jolly's Saloon at 1 Kinloch Street, Dundee, in addition to being a hairdresser's shop, also sold confectionery and had a small lending library. Owned by James Curran and managed by his sister-in-law Mary Curran, it was called 'Jolly's' as James, a deeply religious man, used the initial letters from his motto: 'Jesus Our Lord Loves us Yet'.

On the Friday afternoon following the appearance of the advertisement in the *Courier*, nine-year-old Ina Curran was looking after the shop. At around four o'clock an elegantly dressed woman and a male companion arrived to view the premises. A meeting with James Curran was arranged for that same evening in the flat Mary shared with her tram conductor husband John, at 39 Church Street. Jessie seemed determined to drive a hard bargain but eventually an agreement was reached whereby the shop would change hands for £130. Business completed, John Curran took Jessie to Taybridge Station. Earlier, Mary had been impressed by Jessie's 'continental' air, and when John returned said that perhaps she could be a German spy. John replied that if anyone heard her saying that they would think she was daft!

It would appear that Jessie had some difficulty in raising the money as it was not until 6 September that, following further protracted negotiations, the shop finally passed to Jessie for £70, which she handed to James Curran in crisp new Bank of England £10 notes. Mary Curran was kept on, and Jessie's 15-year-old niece Patricia, daughter of her other stepbrother, Frank Haddow, was taken on as a trainee. This arrangement would give Jessie the freedom she needed to carry on her work for Germany.

Later that month Jessie was back in Hamburg at an Abwehr conference where amongst other things her future role was discussed. Also present at the conference was Ignatz Griebl. It was decided that Jessie's shop would make an excellent cut-out address for mail being sent from America, which she would then either take to Germany herself or hand over to another courier. This arrangement would later be extended to include packets from Abwehr agents in Strasbourg and Czechoslovakia. Strasbourg, on the border between France and Germany, was of considerable strategic importance. From there two renegade French army officers, named Credle and Froge, were selling the secrets of the Maginot Line. Meanwhile Hitler was also intent on destabilising Czechoslovakia which, as a result of the appeasement policies of the British and French governments, would be effectively dismembered only months later by the Munich agreement.

Despite her reputation as a successful business woman, Jessie had initially failed to realise that, instead of a fashionable district of cosmopolitan Hamburg, she was now operating in a working-class district of distinctly unfashionable Dundee. It rapidly became apparent that a perm costing 10/- (50p) was not about to be a market leader in an area where household income averaged less than £4 per week. With the business clearly not doing as well as it might, Jessie's frequent absences began to cause comment. Further, large packets of mail began to arrive, chiefly from America, something which did seem strange to Mary Curran as she had managed to run the shop without such a regular international correspondence.

Mary's first impression of Jessie was confirmed for her when, while tidying the shop, she saw a small piece of paper sticking out from under the linoleum covering the counter. Examining it, she saw it was a drawing of the Tay Rail Bridge which carried the legend 'Zeppelin'. Having decided that she would have to speak to her husband about it, for safety she hid the sketch down the front of her dress. Unsure of what to do, John Curran took the sketch to his boss, Tramway Inspector Pat Robbins. To Mary's frustration, neither her husband nor Pat Robbins were immediately convinced that there was anything to be concerned about.

Shortly afterwards another piece of paper turned up inside the pages of a book which Jessie had left lying under the counter. On it was a series of code letters and again the word 'Zeppelin'. After hastily copying and replacing it, she gave the copy to John who passed in on to Pat Robbins. Robbins was beginning to suspect that there really was something in what Mary had found and passed this latest information to the police early in November.

'Zeppelin' would appear to have been Jessie's code name. Abwehr tended to give its agents rather unfortunate aliases. Wilhelm Lonkowski, arrested in 1935 while trying to board a ship in New York with a violin case full of documents, they had given the code name 'Sex'.

Initially the police reacted in much the same way as had John Curran and Pat Robbins: they were sceptical. The Chief Constable of Perth, who had known the Haddow family for years, thought the very idea of a German spy in Dundee ridiculous. A number of meetings were held over the following two weeks, including interviews with both Robbins and Curran. These were facilitated by the Tramway Depot being next door to the Police Head-quarters and there being a discreet rear access from one to the other. Neither Robbins nor the Currans were keen to have their roles in the affair made public for fear of Nazi reprisals, and Chief Constable Neilans was at pains to reassure them on that point.

By Thursday, 18 November, Neilans felt that the evidence against Jessie was strong enough for the matter to be taken seriously. Around this time a young lecturer in the German Department at the University College, Dr Harry Law Robertson, was interrupted during one of his tutorials by two detectives who asked for his help in interpreting some of the information on a sketch of what they took to be a part of Leuchars Airfield. The documents found at the shop were photographed and replaced in order not to arouse Jessie's suspicions and, armed with copies, Detective Lieutenant John Carstairs was sent on the night train to MI5 headquarters in Cromwell Road, London. Immediately after his meeting the next morning, Carstairs phoned Neilans and told him that the case was 'hot', and that MI5 had requested a watch be kept both on Jessie and on the shop.

That Friday evening John Curran had arranged to meet Mary at the shop before going on to the cinema. Arriving at Kinloch Street he found Mary, as he said later, looking both suspicious and quiet. Earlier Jessie had told them that she was planning a short trip to England; now, however, she announced that she had business in Germany and that she was leaving that very night by boat from Dundee. She asked John to give her a hand with her luggage. She had to be aboard the ship by nine p.m.

Making the excuse that he wanted to wash and change, John hurried to the top of the Hilltown and took a bus into town. On the way to the Tramway Depot he phoned Robbins and asked him to have CID officers in his office when he arrived. Telling them of Jessie's intentions, he was instructed to return to the shop and carry on as normal. He was assured that the police would be watching.

John arrived back at the shop just as Jessie and Mary were locking up at eight-thirty. After catching a bus from the Hilltown to Shore Terrace, all three walked slowly along Dock Street to Camperdown Dock. They were followed by Detective Constable Peter Fletcher and WPC Annie Ross. At Camperdown Dock they boarded the SS *Courland*, one of a pair of vessels owned by the Currie Line, which operated a weekly service between Dundee or Leith and Hamburg carrying mixed cargoes and a small number of passengers. On this occasion part of her cargo, herring coming by train from Aberdeen, was delayed, resulting in the ship missing the tide and being unable to sail until the following day.

Having unexpected time on her hands, Jessie suggested to the Currans that they should all walk along to the buffet at the West Station for a drink. Aware of the CID surveillance operation, John was more concerned that he and Mary should be getting home. In her parting words to the Currans that night Jessie commented ruefully that she had a lot of worries from all corners of the world. 'If only you knew,' she said. The Currans, of course, knew a great deal more than she credited them with! That cold November night Detective Inspector Tom Nicholson had the unenviable task of keeping watch on the ship.

With the *Courland* not due to sail until the early afternoon, Jessie came ashore the following morning and, after shopping at G. L. Wilson's and calling briefly at Kinloch Street, went back on board at midday. When the ship sailed at two-thirty, she became the responsibility of a team of watchers from MI6 as MI5 had no jurisdiction outside British territory. There is some evidence that the delay in the arrival of the herring was arranged to allow MI6 to get a watcher on board. Earlier that evening WPC Ella McFarlane had been told to be prepared to follow Jessie to Hamburg. This was not to prove necessary as a Secret Intelligence Service officer was on board when the ship sailed the next afternoon.

Just how much, if anything, did MI5 know about Jessie Jordan prior to Carstairs' arrival at Cromwell Road that Friday morning?

In the late 1930s, MI5 was monitoring the large numbers of refugees flowing into Britain from Germany, as it was clear that Abwehr would use this human traffic to infiltrate its agents into the country. Given the scale of the problem, this scrutiny was at times somewhat cursory. Jessie, however, made the fundamental error of attracting attention to herself. In 1936 she wrote from Hamburg to Glasgow Police asking for their help in proving Marga's Aryan descent. Early in 1937, shortly after her arrival in Scotland, she visited Glasgow Police Headquarters asking about re-registration as a British citizen, and called there again on her way back from Wales enquiring about her right as a German citizen to operate a business in this country. This last matter eventually took her into correspondence with the Home Office in early September. She even appears in the Perth Directory for 1937/38, albeit as Mrs Jessie Jardine. All of this runs contrary to the accepted wisdom that spies should merge into their surroundings, appearing unremarkable in every way.

In a rather colourful article in the Scottish *Sunday Express* in 1955, Theo Long suggests that she was spotted during her visit to Aldershot in June. Whilst he presents no hard evidence to support this, some circumstantial evidence does point to MI5 having prior knowledge of her activities. Why, for example, were MI5 so readily prepared to accept the case as being 'hot' on the evidence shown to them by John Carstairs, evidence which only days previously the Chief Constables of both Perth and Dundee had regarded with such scepticism? Secondly, any port with regular sailings to Germany was being watched by MI5. In the days before such travel became commonplace anyone making more than one crossing in a short period would certainly attract their interest. What is known is that the policy of Sir Vernon Kell, then Director of MI5, was to leave such agents in place for as long as possible in the hope that they would lead his men to their co-conspirators.

Jessie was away for over a week. On her return she spent the night at the shop and the following morning, clearly worried, she let slip to Mary Curran that she knew her mail had been tampered with. Several days later Mary found the map Jessie had been using to identify coastal installations. This was shown to Neilans on 9 December before being photographed and replaced at the shop.

Meanwhile, things had started to go seriously wrong in America. Gustav Rumrich, a 27-year-old former US army mess sergeant who had deserted after a discrepancy in mess funds had been discovered. He had offered his services as a spy for Germany by writing to Abwehr, c/o the Nazi party newspaper, the *Volkischer Beobachter*. In spite of this unorthodox approach, acceptance of his offer was signalled by a classified advert in the *New York Times* on 6 April 1936, in which 'Theodor Koerner' was asked to contact 'Sanders' at Postbus 629, Hamburg. He became a part of the Griebl organisation and much of the material sent from America was channelled through him to Kinloch Street and then on to Germany.

Rumrich's real motive for betrayal would appear to have been financial. He decided to take advantage of the $1,000 that Hamburg was prepared to pay for some blank American passports which were to be used to infiltrate German agents into the Soviet Union. He booked himself into the Taft Hotel and phoned the chief of the New York office of the State Department Passport Division. Identifying himself as Edward Weston, the Under Secretary of State, he demanded that 50 blank passports be sent to him at the hotel. The passport office official was highly suspicious of this odd request and immediately informed the police. An arrangement was made whereby a clerk would deliver the passports to a messenger in the street outside the hotel. When the messenger, who was of course Rumrich himself, turned up he was immediately arrested and it was his subsequent full confession that brought about the collapse of the ring. Griebl also agreed to co-operate with the FBI and, in February 1938, Johanna Hoffman was detained on board the *Europa* when her cabin was found to contain a large number of secret documents.

For almost 15 weeks MI5 and Dundee Police kept Jessie Jordan under surveillance. In Dundee this involved officers keeping watch on the shop and the bedsit she was renting at 23 Stirling Street, by concealing themselves in closes either at the end of Stirling Street or next to Rough and Fraser's bakery in Kinghorne Road. Local police were used for this as strangers hanging around a small community such as the Hilltown would quickly excite comment. Peter Fletcher, then Detective Constable, remembers that one problem was how to avoid arousing the curiosity of the bookies who used the top of the Hilltown as a place of business.

By the end of February, with the FBI operation in America complete, MI5 were ready to act and on the morning of Wednesday, 2 March, Hinchley Cooke arrived at Police Headquarters in West Bell Street. After consulting the Procurator Fiscal, he and Neilans along with Carstairs and Ross went to the shop, where they arrested Jessie.

Having searched the shop and taken possession of what Neilans described as 'various papers and articles', he along with Cooke, Nicholson and Carstairs searched the flat in Stirling Street. From there the group left for Perth, where they examined the house at Breadalbane Terrace but found nothing of interest. This would have been the first indication for Marga that something was amiss. She had returned from Hamburg with her mother in the previous September to take over as housekeeper at Breadalbane Terrace and was in the flat when Neilans and Cooke arrived. She would always maintain her ignorance of her mother's activities as a spy.

From Perth the group went to Coupar Angus where they searched the house belonging to Patricia Haddow's parents, Frank and Barbara Haddow, at 26 Strathmore Avenue, again finding nothing. Back at Police Headquarters that evening, they interviewed Jessie. At first she attempted to deny everything but one final damning piece of evidence had arrived that very day. At lunchtime a registered letter was delivered to the shop. It was later handed by an officer keeping watch there to Cooke. It contained £25 in consecutively numbered notes. From the MI5 surveillance operation, Cooke was well aware of the letter and its contents. He used this to set a simple trap for Jessie during her subsequent interrogation.

At seven p.m. Jessie was taken down to spend her first night in the cells. She appeared for one minute at the Police Court on the following morning and was remanded until 10 March for further enquiries. Immediately afterwards she was brought back to Neilans' room by Annie Ross. Cooke and Carstairs were also present. She was asked about the money, which she tried to pass off as the repayment of a loan of 300 marks from a Captain Weber. On being questioned by Cooke she did however agree that Weber also called himself Sanders, Otto Mauser and Strattan, aliases already known to MI5 and the FBI. The classified advert placed in the *New York Times* to signal to Gustav Rumrich that his services were required asked him to write to Sanders at a Hamburg box number, also now a known Abwehr address.

She soon admitted that she was receiving the money, which came by post from Amsterdam every month, in return for information on shipping and other matters. She was also questioned about a sketch, which had reached the police through Mary Curran, and which appears to have been an early draft, possibly the original, of that of the depot at Crombie. Having admitted to the fact that she had been asked to make it by Weber she agreed to take Neilans and Cooke to the spot where it had been drawn. They left to catch the morning ferry. Base Security Officer at Crombie, Major Quinlan, was shown the sketch and said that it would be of some assistance to an enemy pilot. He confirmed that it appeared to have been made from a stretch of road known locally as 'Fiddlers Hall', and with this information the party returned to Dundee. Meanwhile, at Kinloch Street, Assistant Chief Constable Pattison was supervising an examination of the drains.

The other major piece of evidence to come from the shop was the map. On Tuesday, 8 March, Neilans took it to Rosyth, where he spoke to the officer commanding, Admiral Thomson, and Commander Brand. They referred him to the Inspector of Coastguards, Captain A. L. Fletcher, whom Neilans and Cooke met the next day at Carnoustie Coastguard Station. He confirmed that the map had been marked to show coastal installations such as batteries at Broughty Ferry and Carnoustie. Further markings on the map included what were described as 'three castles' at Fife Ness, and the Coastguard Stations at Methil and Carnoustie. In the next few days Neilans and Cooke were to visit a number of other locations in Fife and Angus.

In Dundee, a queue for the 20 places in the public benches formed in Court House Square over an hour before Jessie's appearance in the Police Court at ten a.m. on Thursday, 10 March. A crowd also gathered when she was taken to Perth Prison a week later.

In America, four arrests were made, including Rumrich and Hoffman, along with Otto Voss, an aircraft worker, and Erich Glaser, a private in the US army. Griebl escaped to Germany, to turn up during the war as a gynae-cologist in an Aryanised, formerly Jewish, practice in Vienna. A Federal Grand Jury indictment of 21 June that year named 18 people as having spied for the Nazis – including Jessie Jordan.

At the subsequent trial, Rumrich, who was described as a 'beer pitcher and romancer', gave evidence for the prosecution and received a sentence of two years, as did Glaser. Hoffman, described by Justice Knox as a pathetic figure, collapsed in the dock on being given four years in prison and Voss was, in turn, given six years. Much of the evidence for the prosecution was based on letters intercepted by MI5 in Dundee. One of these referred to a scheme to steal the plans of the new aircraft carriers *Yorktown* and *Enterprise*, using counterfeit White House notepaper and the forged signature of President Roosevelt. In his closing remarks Justice Knox spoke of the Germans bungling efforts at espionage, but criticised the FBI for allowing Griebl and one other defendant to escape.

Jessie Jordan appeared before Lord Aitchison at the High Court in Edinburgh on Monday, 16 May 1938. Contemporary newspaper reports describe her as looking pale but calm, elegantly dressed in the same fur-trimmed coat and green hat she had been wearing when she was arrested. Having clearly cooperated fully with her MI5 interrogators, she was able to plead guilty to reduced charges and was sentenced to four years in prison. In marked contrast to her mother's self possession, Marga sat in court looking greatly distressed. After the sentencing she was led in to see Jessie who, despite her own problems, was able to reassure her.

Shortly before her mother's arrest, Marga had been taken to a dance at Perth Barracks by a young salesman from Glasgow, Tom Reid. Throughout the trauma that followed, Tom stood by Marga and, in April 1938, they were married at the Blacksmith's Shop, Gretna Green. It is possible that this marriage, which was later formally registered in Glasgow, may have been bigamous as, when interviewed by Theo Long in 1955, Herman Wobrock denied ever having divorced Marga.

In November, partly to reclaim her furniture for her new home in Glasgow, and partly to escape the attention of the press, Marga sailed for Hamburg for a short break. On 16 January 1939 she wrote to Tom saying that she would be back in a few days. Four days later, aged 25, she was dead, apparently during an emergency operation.

News of Marga's death broke Jessie's spirit. During the war she was transferred to Holloway Prison where she became a Christian Scientist. In 1945 she was repatriated to Germany where she spent the rest of her days as a missionary for that cause. She died in Hannover in November 1954 after refusing medical treatment.

What of the importance of the spy ring and of Jessie's role in it?

At the trial in New York it was said in evidence that 'the conspiracy was furthered by conferences between the defendants in New York, Buffalo, Bremerhaven, Bremen, Berlin, Hamburg, Dundee and Havana'. The FBI stated that the Griebl ring was the greatest spy ring in peacetime history. However, this was said amidst mounting spy hysteria in both Britain and

America, and is in any case somewhat at odds with the remarks made by Justice Knox at the trial in New York.

Jessie Jordan was no mistress of deception. In her role as a spy she was of little value to Germany. Her appreciation of military matters was best illustrated by the description of the installations at Fife Ness as 'three castles'. Potentially, she had far greater value as a courier but was only able to operate as such for, at best, a few weeks before coming under surveillance. By those who knew her she is remembered as being both strong-willed and strict, but capable of great kindness and generosity.

Several aspects of the case are still tantalisingly unclear. Why, for example, when she realised on her return from Hamburg in November 1937 that her mail was being intercepted, did she not make a run for it? Had she been turned by MI5, and was she then being used in a disinformation role similar to that in which most of the German agents caught during the war were employed? Why did she move out of the bedsit at Stirling Street only four days before her arrest, thereafter staying at the shop? Records of the security and intelligence agencies are held under section 3(4) of the Public Records Act 1958 and as such will remain permanently closed to the public.

In Dundee, little time was wasted in auctioning the contents of the shop. As a final irony, at a sale packed with souvenir hunters where even the linoleum was sold for 32/6d (£1.62½), the chief buyer of the shop fittings was ex-Baillie Peter Fletcher, owner of a hairdresser's shop in the Overgate and father of the same Detective Constable Peter Fletcher who had spent so many nights watching their previous owner. The shop itself fell victim to post-war redevelopment, as did the flats at Stirling Street and Church Street along with the Tramway Depot and the old Police Headquarters in West Bell Street. At Camperdown Dock, the north wall from where the *Courland* sailed that Saturday afternoon in November 1937 is now the depository for a large heap of rusting scrap metal. At Breadalbane Terrace in Perth the old railway flats have long since disappeared, the only sign of their existence being the weed-infested pavement extending past the site of the close at number 16.

It is however still possible to walk the short distance from Charleston village in Fife to the stretch of road overlooking the depot at Crombie, a scene quite unchanged after more than half a century. Once there, it is easy to bring to one's mind's eye the image of a stocky, middle-aged woman looking nervously about her on that spring day in 1937, hastily scribbling . . . and hurrying away.

Chapter Two

'One in the Eye for Old Adolf!'

Home Front 1938–1940

It had been raining. An eerie silence had settled over the city centre that Sunday morning, 3 September 1939, as H. Samuel's clock at the corner of Reform Street moved slowly towards 11.15. 'This morning, the British Ambassador in Berlin handed the German government a final note stating that unless . . . and consequently this country is at war with Germany.' Within an hour of Neville Chamberlain's dispirited announcement armed policemen had sealed off Court House Square and men in uniform were making their way to Taybridge Station. Many would not see their city for six years, some would never return. Dundee had gone to war.

As excitement over the Jordan affair began to die down in the summer of 1938, attention turned to the looming crisis over Czechoslovakia and visits to the Empire Exhibition in Glasgow. With an impeccable sense of timing, almost one month to the day before Munich, Dundee Corporation were discussing their territorial demands in Fife, namely a plan to annexe Newport and Wormit. In the *Sunday Mail*, Robert Brown, the newly appointed Air Raid Precautions Officer for Dundee, was reported as seeking 800 volunteer Air Raid Wardens.

An attempt to hold a fascist meeting in City Square that summer was thwarted by a large crowd of hostile Dundonians. The speaker was to have been a Mr Chambers-Hunter, the prospective British Union Party candidate for Aberdeen North. He was last seen giving fascist salutes from the open roof of his car as it was pursued up Reform Street.

Munich had brought a short-lived respite but, by August 1939, the outbreak of war was simply a matter of time. On 9 August the *Courier* editorial stated: 'It is very plain today that if the German economic system is to survive, it must steadily be fed by the acquisition of new territory.' That morning the Scottish National Service of the BBC was broadcasting live from a rain-lashed

Sunday, 3 September 1939, at 11.12 a.m. by the clock on H. Samuel's, 'The Empire's Largest Jewellers', and the streets are wet from thundery showers. Outside the City Chambers are cars belonging to members of the Emergency Committee of the Corporation, at that very moment adjourning their deliberations on accommodation for Auxiliary Firemen in order to listen to the Prime Minister's broadcast on the outbreak of war. Almost the only other people on the streets that morning are a smaller than usual number of church-goers, some of whom will hear the sombre news from the pulpit.

DUNDEE COURIER AND EVENING TELEGRAPH

Weymouth Bay, where the King was reviewing the 12,000 men and 133 ships of the reserve fleet of the Royal Navy. Two days later, HMS *Forth*, the depot ship of the Second Submarine Flotilla arrived in the Tay with six of her charges. She was joined soon after by a cargo vessel which was treated with considerable respect; it was carrying the first of the mines that would be laid off the estuary.

On Monday, 14 August, Gillies & Co. were proud to announce that Lord and Lady Provost Phin would attend the opening of their new shop in Broughty Ferry, and at Bonneville Salt Flats in America, John Cobb was about to attempt a new land speed record in his Napier Railton. The new Tay Ferry *Abercraig* was nearing completion at Elderslie that week and the Caledon

Shipyard was celebrating the successful trials of the new lighthouse tender, *Hesperus*. In the *Courier*, 'Aunt Kate' was urging women to preserve fruits and pickles, and to make their own jam, cheese and butter. In *Woman's Welcome* one could read the story of a woman's terrible experiences in Germany in 'Married to a Nazi'.

That Saturday, as feverish efforts were being made to persuade the Polish Government to compromise with Germany over Danzig, Dundee F.C. beat Airdrie 3-2 at Broomfield, leaving them top of the league.

On Monday, 22 August, British citizens were warned to leave Poland. The following day the Nazi-Soviet pact was announced and the Government took emergency powers. In Dundee, livestock sales were suffering from poor attendances and low prices, and farmers were concerned that a possible shortage of manpower would lead to difficulties with the 'tattie lifting'. The

The army had, for many years, provided an escape route from the chronic male unemployment which bedevilled Dundee. As war clouds gather, Sergeant L. Simpson cuts an imposing figure at a National Service recruitment booth outside Burton's in City Square.
DUNDEE COURIER AND EVENING TELEGRAPH

LNER were offering third class return trips from Taybridge Station to the Morecambe illuminations for 24/6d (£1.22½) and at Lamb's Garage in Trades Lane a new Austin Eight cost £128 ex-works. That weekend, sheepdog trials were being held at Tayport and Invergowrie and the Alhambra Cinema in Bellfield Street was showing *Shopworn Angel*, a melodrama starring Margaret Sullivan and James Stewart, along with *Blazing Terror* starring Wild Bill Hickock. The Dundee Registrar was reporting a five-fold increase in the marriage rate, one couple having roused him from his bed at two a.m. as the groom had to rejoin his ship, HMS *Exeter*, later that morning.

In honour of the 3,900 delegates from the British Association for the Advancement of Science holding their annual conference in Dundee that week, City Square had been laid out with lawns and flower beds. One of the delegates at the British Association was Sir William Beveridge, later to be the architect of the welfare state. Another, Miss Mary Ellis, was due to address the Psychology Section on a study of the sorting process in laundries. On Friday, 1 September, Sir Albert Seward, President of the B.A., opened the Dundee Flower Show at the new Ice Rink on the Kingsway. The previous evening, as a reception was being held in the Caird Hall to welcome the delegates, staff in the Education Department offices in Castle Street worked into the night, often assisted by guests in their evening clothes, to pack food for the first batch of evacuees due to leave the following day.

Despite pouring rain, football went ahead as usual on Saturday, Dundee drawing 1-1 with Morton at Cappielow and Dundee United going down 2-0 to Leith Athletic. D. M. Brown's were offering afternoon and evening gowns for 63/- (£3.15), and it is to be hoped that Hitler was unaware that their restaurant was the 'favourite rendezvous in Dundee' where a table d'hôte lunch could be had for 1/6d (7½p).

The imminence of war could not be avoided though; the blackout had begun the previous night and, on that last morning of peace, the *Courier* stated in an editorial entitled 'WAR' that '. . . we are to confront this German pestilence'. Sandbags were appearing at close mouths, over plate glass windows and around public buildings; 117,000 at Court House Square alone. Windows were criss-crossed with anti-shatter tape or covered with Celotex blackout material, and yellow gas detector boards were being fixed to lamp posts. All the city's cinemas, theatres, dance halls, tennis courts, bowling and putting greens were facing closure. Morgan and Grove Academies were cancelling plans for their jubilee celebrations, and Lord Provost Phin was appealing for blood donors. In great haste, Corporation workmen were painting the corners of buildings, trees, the edges of pavements and lamp posts with white stripes to make them more visible in the blackout. That this was being done by Corporation workmen rather than time-served men brought a protest from the Dundee Federation of Master Painters.

On the wireless at eight o'clock that night, as the last shreds of hope for peace disappeared, Tommy Trinder with Geraldo and his Orchestra were valiantly trying to raise the spirits of listeners to 'Up with the Curtain'. Within hours the hopes of a generation which lived through the First World War, the 'war to end all wars' which had claimed the lives of over 4,000 Dundonians, would be dashed for ever.

For the civilian population the Second World War would be above all a time of movement. Vast numbers would be travelling at any one time as either refugees, internees, evacuees, civilian workers or as members of the armed services. Apart from the departure of members of the armed services, the first great migration took place on the morning of Friday, 1 September, with the start of evacuation. It was planned that 11,452 schoolchildren, accompanied children under five, expectant mothers and the blind would leave Dundee on the first day, followed by a further 13,123 on the Saturday. For the previous fortnight, mothers had been laying siege to the Air Raid Precautions Department office in Shore Terrace demanding information on the evacuation scheme. One woman is said to have demanded 'a ticket for meh bairn tae the ARP picnic'.

The fact that only 8,800 turned up over the two days was fortuitous as the Scottish Office had been aware since the previous year that there was nowhere near enough accommodation in the receiving areas. Many of those who did go found the extra holiday from school, which had restarted only the previous week, very welcome. For others the emotional trauma was too great and a drift back to the city began almost immediately. Less than 24 hours after the first evacuees had left, one Dundee Baillie was in Banchory attempting to dissuade a large number from returning. By 9 September the *Courier* was reporting that amongst the reasons given by returning evacuees were, 'they country folk a' live on parritch, bread and butter', and 'I'm feart o' yon coos!'. By mid-November, 74% of the mothers and children evacuated from Dundee had returned to the city.

For some evacuees the story was one of considerable discomfort; one child evacuated to Perth was found to have been forced to sleep in a shed. For others, a clean bed made up with sheets was one of many new experiences, as were a balanced diet and a table laid with cutlery. Within three days of the

31

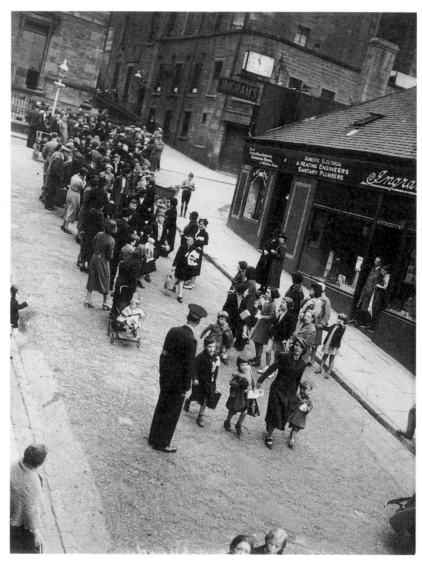

Friday, 1 September 1939 at 11.00 a.m. and evacuees from Victoria Road School assemble in Kings Road prior to making their way to Dundee East Station. Ingram's have given over one window to an ARP display. No sooner had the children left than new occupants were moving into their schools. Along with Dudhope Castle, Butterburn School on Strathmartine Road was taken over by the 5th Battalion Black Watch. The County Battalion took over as Dundee Garrison when the 4th Battalion (Dundee's Ain) became one of the first units to leave for France.

DUNDEE COURIER AND EVENING TELEGRAPH

first evacuation Angus County Council were complaining to Dundee about the number of children who had arrived covered in lice, undernourished and with insufficient clothes. In Crieff, half of the children received were verminous, and at Montrose almost a third of the children who stayed beyond the first days had to be treated for infectious diseases. Urgent appeals for warm clothing were put out and, in some extreme cases, evacuees were simply sent back to the city.

What this first evacuation did achieve was to bring home forcibly to the more affluent and better fed residents of rural areas the true level of inner city decay and deprivation. This was a factor which would have a considerable impact on post-war housing and welfare policies. Similarly, many evacuees gained for the first time a clear understanding of the social inequalities of pre-war Britain. Despite this, when a further evacuation was proposed in 1940 the *Perthshire Advertiser* reported a strong view amongst its readership that receiving families should have a say in where their evacuees came from. When the second evacuation was announced, Perthshire was told to be ready to accept 10,000 new evacuees. This led to protests from the County Council and, following an appeal for accommodation which was largely ignored, the possibility of compelling households to accept children. In the event the scheme foundered as by then the vast majority of the city's population had returned and the schools had almost all reopened. As the *People's Journal* put it at the time, 'Scotland won't stand for it again'.

Another view, expressed in the correspondence column of the *Perthshire Advertiser*, was that evacuees should be 'kept in camps'. As a belated and inadequate response to the shortage of accommodation in the receiving areas, in February 1939 the Scottish Special Housing Association was commissioned to construct camps near each of the five evacuable areas in Scotland. The camp for Dundee was built near Meigle at Belmont Castle and eventually completed in April 1940. By November 1940 a Scottish Education Department official was reporting that the camp had become 'a costly business to run', with a headmaster, ten teachers and 21 'other ranks' being required to look after 124 children. He noted that children were selected for the camp 'except those known to be carrying disease, bedwetters (this only discernable after trial) and difficult'. What he referred to as decent and hopeful children had been withdrawn and by then Belmont Camp contained 'a very large majority of "C" children to whom the malicious damage is probably due'.

The role of the camp was also being questioned as there was no clear statement of priorities between evacuation, physical fitness and education.

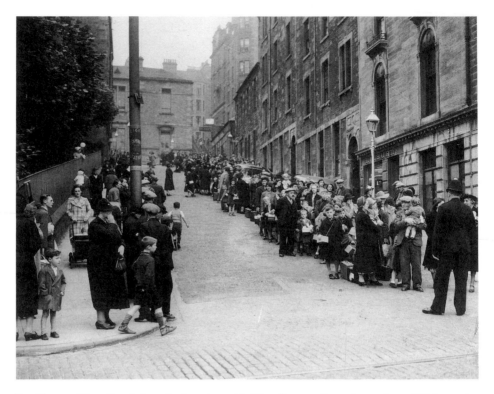

Looking up Kings Road from its junction with King Street a few minutes later. With massive destruction from air attack expected within days or even hours, many of the parents are showing clear signs of apprehension and distress. By this time most members of the reserve forces had already left and family life would never be quite the same again.
DUNDEE COURIER AND EVENING TELEGRAPH

This was further complicated by a conflict of interest between the S.S.H.A., who were responsible for the domestic arrangements, and the Local Authority Education Department whose staff were required to educate and look after the children. In May 1941 the camp contained only 64 children and the Scottish Office wanted to use the space to provide accommodation for children from other areas such as Clydebank which had just suffered heavy bombing that had left many homeless. Dundee Corporation refused, stating that they would send 100 children from the city.

Those who could afford it sent their children accompanied, should they so wish, by their mothers and nurses or governesses to Canada. In doing so they were following in the footsteps of at least three MPs who had fled to North

America by July 1940. In response to public demand the Government reluctantly instituted an official overseas evacuation scheme in June, though this was soon overwhelmed, an embarrassing 210,000 applications having been received in two weeks, 900 of which were from Dundee. The sinking of the *Arandora Star* on 2 July allowed the Cabinet to temporarily suspend the scheme. Overseas evacuation however was quietly resumed in August, continuing until 18 September when the *City of Benares* was sunk 600 miles out into the Atlantic. The fact that only 13 of the 90 children on board survived, along with 82 of the crew, convinced the War Cabinet to announce another 'temporary suspension' of the scheme although it had in fact been abandoned.

Fourth Officer of the *City of Benares* was 22-year-old Ronald Cooper from Invergowrie who took command of a lifeboat containing 46 survivors including six children. After eight days they were spotted by a Sunderland from 10 Squadron AAF based at Oban and picked up by the destroyer HMS *Anthony*. Cooper received a hero's welcome when he returned to Dundee on Friday, 28 September, and was later awarded the MBE.

One of the 14 children from Dundee on the *Arandora Star* was nine-year-old Sheila Caswell from North Wellington Street. Phlegmatic about her experience, she told a *Courier* reporter that they had not really been excited, and that 'the only thing that bothered us was the biscuits we got to eat in the lifeboat. My sister Theresa didn't like them much, they were hard.'

The blackout had begun in Dundee, as elsewhere, on Friday, 1 September, with initially very poor results; both the RAF and the *Courier* were taking photographs showing the city's streets ablaze with light. During the first week of the war a *People's Journal* reporter noted that while the city centre and the west end were completely in darkness, the area bounded by Lochee, Strathmore Avenue, Strathmartine Road and the top of the Hilltown contained the worst offenders. ARP serge blackout cloth was available from Barnet's in City Square in navy, nigger or dark green at 2/9d (14½p) per yard. One of a series of Civil Defence leaflets issued by the Government the previous July had lectured sternly on the need for an effective blackout, but a survey showed that less than a third of people had even bothered to read them.

In August 1940 one Dundonian making his way home in the blackout was caught using an unshaded torch in Tally Street. On being hauled up before Sheriff Malcolm the next morning, he was told that enemy planes were looking for the lights of these torches and were being guided by them. He was fined £1 for the blackout offence and £2 for resisting the police. The

Heavy, thundery showers on Saturday, 2 September only added to the misery and bewilderment clearly visible in this picture taken outside the Town Hall in Kirriemuir.
DUNDEE COURIER AND EVENING TELEGRAPH

following week, Sheriff Malcolm asked one resident of Princes Street, who had accidentally shown a light while getting dressed after the sirens sounded, if his attitude to the Germans was 'don't drop any bombs till I get my trousers on'? That Christmas, Margaret Todd of 194 Broughty Ferry Road was sent to prison for ten days after showing lights from her house on two consecutive nights. On both occasions she had barricaded the door to stop the police getting in, and on the second night they had to break down part of a wall to arrest her.

Despite many such early problems the blackout soon became total and was rigidly enforced. One visitor to the city in 1942 wrote that, while travelling from Blackness to Downfield, he had not seen a single chink of light. Though the aim was to make the city invisible from the air, the effect was also to make Dundee invisible to those on the ground. Pedestrians were in considerable danger at night as, for example, the city's trams could often be heard before being seen and, despite the reduction in traffic brought about by petrol rationing, road accidents increased sharply. So dark was it that, at Newport Pier, a naval Petty Officer was drowned after walking the wrong way off the Tay Ferry *Abercraig* and falling into the river.

Hand torches had been reduced to a narrow beam and had their reflectors removed, the result being described as about as much use as carrying a red hot nail. Cars were allowed only one headlamp fitted with a shade which reduced its effectiveness to almost nil. Despite this they were banned from the Law Hill at night as it was believed that the steep angle of the road might make even this feeble glow visible to an aircraft. A house in Downfield had to be broken into by police after the family had gone out during the day leaving all the lights on and, in the west end, a householder who refused to respond to a warden's request to darken a window found that his next visitor was a policeman who walked straight in and smashed the offending gas mantle.

In addition to the blackout, the Corporation were concerned that the Law Monument and the whitewashed cottages at Broughty Ferry would attract German bombers to the city. The Law Monument was concealed behind camouflage constructed of wood and canvas, though this was set on fire one night in early October with the resulting blaze being visible for miles. As it was even felt that a passing German pilot would be able to recognise Victoria and Stobsmuir ponds, they were filled in. What the Corporation intended to do to camouflage Dundee's most visible landmark which pointed like an arrow straight at the heart of the city, namely the Tay Bridge, is not recorded.

At Glamis Castle, the Earl of Strathmore, whose estate cottages were famous for the brilliance of their annually applied whitewash, refused to have them camouflaged. As a compromise, however, he did agree not to repaint them until the end of the war.

Following the evacuation, the next mass movement of people out of Dundee took place in the days that followed the entry of Italy into the war on Monday, 10 June 1940. Under a heading in February 1940 which asked 'Is the aliens net closed?', the *People's Journal* stated that there were 404 persons on the Aliens Register in Dundee, including 20 Germans of whom one had been interned, the rest being regarded either as harmless or as 'victims of Nazi oppression'. The issue died down as the phoney war dragged on, but resurfaced with Hitler's invasion of Norway in April 1940. There were 229 Italians on the register in the city and heated arguments were

Evacuation was an experience which left little room for dignity. Each evacuee was labelled and issued with a brown carrier bag containing food for the journey in which poorer families, who did not possess hand luggage, were often reduced to carrying their belongings. Much ill feeling was generated when it was discovered that largely middle-class receiving families were being given an allowance of as much as 10/6d (52½p) per week for each child taken in whilst the children of unemployed families qualified for a maximum allowance of 3/- (15p) and those of servicemen 5/- (25p).
DUNDEE COURIER AND EVENING TELEGRAPH

taking place between young Dundonians and young Italians over the issue of conscription. There were groundless suggestions being made that young British-born Italians were attempting to take up their father's nationality in order to avoid conscription into the British army. Two further Germans had been interned and it was reported that, despite being implacably opposed to and having suffered at the hands of fascism, the rest were being kept under very close surveillance. In response to harassment many shops felt obliged to put up signs saying the owners were British-born and, only a week prior to registering for service in the British army, one Dundee Italian was quoted as saying, 'I act British, I think British, in fact I *AM* British'.

In the early hours of Tuesday, 11 June approximately 100 un-naturalised Italians were rounded up in Dundee, many being taken from their beds. Herded into police cells at Bell Street, where they were held before being taken to Saughton Prison in Edinburgh, many Italian Scots were taken to the Isle of Man and others found themselves on ships heading for internment camps in Canada. 714 internees, many of them refugees from fascism, drowned when the *Arandora Star* was sunk by a U-boat on 2 July 1940.

Later that week a further 180 who were either un-naturalised or of Italian stock were summarily ordered out of the city, which had been designated a protected zone, and told not to return within 20 miles of it without permission. Against this order, from which the only exceptions were invalids and the infirm along with British-born widows and divorcees, there was no appeal. One Dundee internee was to be so traumatised by the experience of internment that he spent the rest of his life in psychiatric care. Another, a 50-year-old woman ordered out of the city, took accommodation at Ballinluig near Pitlochry, only to find that her cottage was on the wrong side of the river and therefore in a protected zone. Taken to court in Perth, she appeared considerably distressed and was admonished, though her landlord was fined £1 for not informing the police of her presence. On occasion, permission was given to visit relatives in the city who were in many cases home on leave from service with the British armed forces, though anyone caught overstaying the time limit on these visits would be jailed.

The Government attempted to justify this hasty and ill-conceived move on the grounds that it was designed to protect the aliens from hostile public opinion. In reality it was a panic reaction to hysteria centred on the supposed existence of a widespread enemy fifth column. At first, letters on the subject in the *Courier* correspondence column expressed such sentiments as 'collar the lot' and 'a penny spent in these people's shops wounds an allied soldier'. Soon, however, public disquiet grew as distressing tales of personal tragedy and petty inhumanity inflicted on defenceless people began to surface. In an effort to maintain the public facade that it had been a well thought out policy, starting in October 1940 the Government permitted only gradual releases from internment. The episode remains one of the most thoroughly lamentable of the war.

In marked contrast to the treatment meted out to the Italians was that given to the many wartime visitors to the city. The first group of foreign soldiers to arrive in Dundee were units of the Polish army which had

Accompanied by their teacher Miss Noble, children from Ancrum Road School walk to Lochee Station on Saturday, 2 September before being evacuated to Kirriemuir. Immediately in front of Miss Noble and looking at the camera are John and Helen McIntosh aged nine and seven respectively. Behind Helen is Richard Leslie and, behind him, the two girls in cloche hats are from a children's home in Coupar Street. The massive upheaval caused by evacuation led to the temporary abandonment of the principle of compulsory education. Whilst teachers accompanying evacuee children were able to keep up some rudimentary form of education, in the city all the schools were closed and literally thousands of children were left to fend for themselves. This situation was made progressively worse in the ensuing weeks as mothers and children returned to the city and many parents resorted to setting up unofficial schools in their homes. As shelters were built, the schools did begin to reopen but it would be six months before the system returned to anything like normal.

DUNDEE COURIER AND EVENING TELEGRAPH

reformed in Scotland after the campaigns in Poland and France. They had been made responsible for the defence of the coastlines of Angus and Fife.

Amongst the earliest arrivals was a group of sappers who established the Polish Engineering Cadet School in Tay Street School. For these young men 1,000 miles from home, the sight of local people coming to the gate within hours of their arrival and inviting them to their homes was particularly welcome. In those first hours strong bonds were forged, many of which survive to this day.

The Poles had an immediate effect on the social life of the city, making a considerable impression on the local girls with their smart uniforms and impeccable manners. Whilst the phenomenon of someone clicking their heels and bowing during that famous Dundee courting ritual, the 'Monkey Parade', or at the High Street coffee stall may have found favour with the girls, it did not have the same effect on the local men. As one put it, 'the allies were not quite so allied when it came to competing for the local talent'! Asked whether he was concerned at the number of relationships being struck up between Polish servicemen and local girls, the Regional Commissioner for Scotland, Lord Rosebery, replied with characteristic good humour, 'It's none of *my* affair, ho ho!'

Some found novel ways of making money from these new arrivals. One city-centre licensed grocers employed a member of staff to remove the labels from bottles of tonic wine and replace them with ones describing the contents as port!

The Poles were soon joined by French, Dutch, Norwegian, American and Russian servicemen and, between April 1942 and June 1943, the Church of Scotland Hostel in Dudhope Street would provide 10,000 beds for visiting servicemen. Whilst language difficulties could usually be got round, there were occasional problems. On one occasion, a convoy of lorries full of Polish soldiers became split up while going up Lochee Road in the blackout. The resultant chaos as lost drivers who could not speak English attempted to ask directions and police cars roamed all over the west end like sheep dogs searching for strays had apparently to be seen to be believed.

The presence of these fighting men in the city did however provide a visible measure of the true scale of the military disaster that had taken place in Europe. Morale in the city had fluctuated much in line with the rest of the country since the war began. An early sense of purpose, tinged with a sense of resignation, had given way to widespread sullen boredom as war became a series of inconveniences. Hard on the heels of evacuation and the blackout came a budget which put 1d (½p) each on beer, cigarettes and sugar, and raised income tax to 7/6d (38p) in the £1. In Dundee swingeing cuts had been made in public transport. Though tram services were unaffected, bus services had been cut by 50% with the last bus leaving the city centre at ten-thirty p.m. on weekdays and ten p.m. on Sundays. By April 1940, with petrol rationing having compounded the problem and following a number of ill-tempered incidents, the Corporation were forced to erect crush barriers to control the crowds waiting for buses at Shore Terrace.

Those involved in war work were not immune from the effects of muddle and indecision in the early days of war. At the Caledon Shipyard a massive effort had been made to rush the completion of the SS *Glengyle* as an armed merchant cruiser, effectively a warship. No sooner had a navy crew been allocated to her than policy was changed and she reverted to being a defensively equipped merchant ship and the crew was withdrawn. In his war diary the Naval Officer in Charge Dundee described this decision as having had a catastrophic effect on the morale of the workforce. In the event this ship was taken up by the Admiralty and, as HMS *Glengyle*, had a distinguished career as an assault ship in the Mediterranean and at the D-Day landings.

After six months of military inactivity during which the *People's Journal* had been forced to rely heavily on tales of derring-do from the First World War, fiction was suddenly replaced by the real thing. On 11 May 1940, the day after he invaded Holland, Belgium and France, 'Hitler . . . will have to face the greatest army the world has ever seen'. Only five days later, the French army began to collapse and the newly appointed Prime Minister, Winston Churchill, was in Paris attempting to boost morale. The true scale of the impending military disaster began to unfold publicly for the first time that night on the BBC nine o'clock news.

On 18 May the *Journal* urged, 'Be Patient! Our plans will succeed', and reassured its readers that 'Allies fight Germans to a standstill'. Somewhat plaintively on 25 May, as the British Expeditionary Force began its headlong retreat to the Channel, 'They're smiling over there, so why should we lack faith?' Without much conviction on 8 June, five days after the end of the evacuation at Dunkirk and on the very day that the aircraft carrier HMS *Glorious* and two destroyers were sunk while covering the evacuation from Narvik, 'Confidence in Somme battle outcome', and on 15 June, as the French Government asked to be allowed to make a separate peace with Germany, 'Thumbs up and down with gloom'.

42

Among the older children evacuated on Saturday, 2 September were these Harris Academy pupils seen outside Bank Street School in Brechin.
DUNDEE COURIER AND EVENING TELEGRAPH

In the face of an effective news blackout the press was already switching its attention to the home front with extensive coverage of the formation of the Local Defence Volunteers and ARP exercises in City Square, at which members of Dundee Dramatic Society used their make-up talents in the application of fake head wounds.

In mid-1940 the Government took wide-ranging new powers of censorship which included the mass-interception of letters, telegrams and telephone calls both as a measure of public opinion and in order to identify those spreading defeatism. The results of this surveillance, along with those from wider public opinion polling, were used by the Ministry of Information in the preparation of a daily briefing paper on the state of popular morale. As the collapse in France gathered momentum, reports for the east coast including the Dundee area speak of increasing public depression and bewilderment. Despite this, in June it was noted that the general public in Dundee were still 'not sufficiently alive to the seriousness of the situation'. In general, once the shock of defeat had worn off, morale improved, although in July 1940 there was 'much comment on Tayside at the failure of our fighters to engage German raiders . . .' An explanation was sought. In August and September it was reported that there was widespread fear of invasion on the east coast, except in Dundee where there was confidence in the Royal Navy.

There is evidence that alcohol consumption in Dundee increased sharply when morale was at its lowest. On 15 September 1939 Chief Constable Neilans told the City Magistrates that drunkenness during the 12 days since the outbreak of war had been 'phenomenal'. Later he reported that during the first four months of 1940 there had been a 50% increase in 'drunkenness and offences committed while under the influence of drink'. At the same meeting the Rev. Harold Ross was concerned that 'if an alert should come during the blackout, confusion would arise if intoxicated men tried to get into public shelters'.

In rural districts around the city, life continued much as before, despite farmers' complaints that 'townies' employed on erecting anti-invasion defences were trampling much needed crops. The Burrelton and Woodside War Work Committee were knitting for the troops and raising money for the wool fund from the sale of snowdrops. In Perth, the Bishop of St Andrews acknowledged the success of a charity garden fête by stating that it was 'One in the eye for old Adolf!'

City Square – War Weapons Week, February 1941. A symbol of defiance – or phyrric victory?
DUNDEE COURIER AND EVENING TELEGRAPH

This Messerschmitt 109 was shot down at Langenhoe Wick in Essex at 1700 hrs on Tuesday, 29 October 1940, two days prior to the official end of the Battle of Britain, while taking part in a raid on North Weald airfield. (The pilot, Oberfw. Hummeling, was slightly injured and taken prisoner.) It was immediately put to work in the unlikely role of promoting savings campaigns designed to reduce Britain's war debts which were spiralling out of control.

By the late summer of 1940, the war was costing the Exchequer over £10,000,000 per day, a figure which was to rise by a further two millions per day by November. At midday on Thursday, 22 August the War Cabinet listened with mounting horror as the Chancellor, Sir Kingsley Wood, spelt out the stark reality that Britain's gold reserves had fallen from £380 million to £290 million in the previous six weeks and that the country would be effectively bankrupt by the end of the year. A massive and unsustainable Balance of Payments deficit of £2,232,399,000 was forecast for 1940/41 despite dramatic increases in domestic taxation. The Cabinet was sharply divided as to what should be Britain's future policy with some ministers, in particular the Foreign Secretary Lord Halifax and his deputy R. A. 'Rab' Butler, actively pursuing peace feelers behind the backs of ministerial colleagues.

The façade of imperial greatness had, in the space of a mere three months, cracked wide open to reveal a sorry picture of decline and impotence.

The reality of Britain's strategic position was that the Empire was largely defenceless and dominions such as Australia were bluntly informing London that they saw their future security being provided, not by the Royal Navy, but by the American fleet. At home, the remnant of Britain's small army which had survived evacuation from France and Belgium was dangerously ill-equipped, and the cost of replacements was crippling an already weak economy. Trade routes to far-flung parts of the Empire vital to, for example, Dundee's jute industry, were proving impossible for the Navy to adequately protect with its obsolete battleships, and were being slowly strangled. Desperate measures were considered in an effort to halt this collapse. In order to secure the use of the so-called 'treaty ports' in Eire for the Royal Navy, along with a possible Irish entry into the war on the British side, Britain quickly forgot its pledges to the Unionist community and offered the Dublin government a united Ireland. Fearing British duplicity and unwilling to end its neutral stance, the Irish government rejected this proposal.

A plan to offer the Argentinian government sovereignty over the Falkland Islands in return for secure supplies of beef and grain was considered but not pursued.

Other measures under consideration as the situation became daily more grave included the requisitioning of all gold ornaments and wedding rings, although this was not expected to raise more than £20 million.

Two days before the 22 August meeting, in his famous 'Never in the field of human conflict' speech, Churchill had told the House of Commons that Britain must prepare 'resolutely and methodically' for the campaigns of 1941 and 1942. At the end of a fifty-minute speech which, contrary to popular mythology, was never broadcast, he did, however, acknowledge that 'this process means that these two great organisations of the English-speaking democracies, the British Empire and the United States, will have to be somewhat mixed up together in some of their affairs for mutual and general advantage'.

Despite Churchill's attempts to romanticise this 'special relationship', analysts in America were taking a more cynical view based purely on considerations of self-interest. Between June and December 1940 the predominant view was that Britain had lost the war and that America was ideally placed to pick up the pieces of the Empire. American policy changed at the end of the year but resulted in the 'Lend-Lease' scheme by which America swept up all Britain's tangible assets and secured their future world economic dominance.

On 12 November 1940 Lord Lothian, the British Ambassador in Washington, wrote, 'It is only a question of weeks before the resources we have available with which to pay for our requirements and the munitions ordered from the United States are exhausted. Unless we can get financial assistance from the United States on the largest scale, it is obvious that our ability to carry on the war on the current basis must abruptly come to an end'.

Britain ceased to be an independent nation at the end of December 1940 when, without previously consulting London and in a move likened by Churchill to 'a sheriff collecting the last assets of a helpless debtor', Washington despatched a warship to Cape Town to collect the last tangible British assets: £50 million in gold.

Chapter Three

'Civil Defence – The Business of the Citizen'

(CIVIL DEFENCE RECRUITING SLOGAN, 1939)

The Politics of Protection

On 16 July 1940, Major Barclay Brown, the Regional Air Raid Precautions Inspector for Scotland at the Ministry of Home Security, wrote to David Latto, Dundee's Town Clerk, referring to the 'serious deficiency in Dundee of domestic shelters', and the dissatisfaction of his department with the progress being made by the city. He stated that, as a result, the Ministry could 'not accept responsibility in respect of persons killed or wounded' in air raids on the city.

This letter well reflects the exasperation felt by officials in London, Edinburgh and Dundee over the lack of any willingness on the part of the City Corporation to take seriously their share of responsibility to protect the citizens from air attack. It was an issue which would rumble on for six years during which indifference and incompetence would combine with rampant bureaucracy in the disillusionment of many skilled and dedicated people. Further, there would be glaring deficiencies in the protection to which the people of the city were entitled, particularly at the time when the risk of attack was at its greatest.

As war became increasingly likely in the late 1930s it became obvious that, with the advent of long range air power, this would be a war where the front line could be drawn on the doorstep of every home in Britain. This was a new concept to a nation more used to fighting its wars in pursuit of imperial ambition in distant parts of the world. In response to what would be total war and, with the graphic newsreel pictures of the bombing of Guernica during the Spanish Civil War in mind and haunted by images of gas warfare in the trenches, the Government set about the creation of a system whereby the population would be protected and controlled during the massive air strikes which it was believed would follow within hours of a declaration of war.

Filling sandbags at St Andrews in 1939. Great holes appeared in beaches along the river as Corporation workmen filled literally hundreds of thousands of sandbags as a defence against blast and shrapnel. In addition, at weekends, local families were loading their own sandbags – which cost 33/6d (£1.67½p) per 100 – on to barrows and into cars as they created gasproof 'refuge rooms' in their homes. Pubs, with their large plate-glass windows, were a particular cause for concern and, as they disappeared behind 15-foot-high walls of sand, the ARP Committee came to the conclusion that, during a raid, 'pub doors should be closed and no further customers admitted'. Almost immediately vandals took to slashing the sacks with knives, leaving behind piles of wet sand and rotting jute. By April 1940 Dundee Corporation had given up the unequal struggle of trying to keep the sandbags in order and had begun replacing them with 13½-inch thick blast walls of brick.
COWIE COLLECTION, UNIVERSITY OF ST ANDREWS LIBRARY

The Corporation's at best ambivalent attitude to ARP was first demonstrated in January 1936 when it decided by 16 votes to 15 not to send a representative to a first meeting of Local Authorities with the Home Office ARP Department despite the fact that it was being held in the Lesser Caird Hall. Four months later the Police and Fire Committee refused to send a police officer on anti-gas training even though the entire cost was to have been met by the Exchequer. This decision was overturned in May at a meeting of the whole Corporation, but only on the casting vote of the Lord

Provost, Sir John Phin. That summer, the Firemaster asked the Police and Fire Committee for four practice incendiary bombs for training purposes. His request was turned down unless 'the Government undertook to pay the whole expense which would be incurred'. Later, in December 1937, one member stated at a Corporation meeting that none of the city's money should be spent on ARP. In the late summer of 1939 this same member led a motion, defeated by 14 votes to eight, condemning the call up of Territorials. In 1945 he accepted an OBE for services to Dundee in wartime.

The Air Raid Precautions Act became law in January 1938 and placed a range of responsibilities on local authorities. In Dundee it led to the formation of a special sub-committee of the Corporation 'anent Air Raid Precautions' and the appointment, on 18 March, of Police Inspector Robert Brown as ARP Officer. He was given an office in what had been the Lord Provost's parlour and the unenviable task of setting up the network of Civil Defence services required, from nothing, with next to nothing.

In February 1938 the Corporation had placed before it the motion: 'The Town Council, while realising the necessity of taking every possible measure to protect the citizens of Dundee from the effects of aerial bombardment, expresses its conviction that the only complete protection against such attacks is the total abolition of military and naval aviation'. Whilst even with hindsight hopelessly optimistic, this does serve to illustrate the unwillingness to accept the true gravity of the situation in Europe which prevailed throughout the country at the time, and which would eventually lead to the débâcle at Munich later that year. Similar motions were debated by many other authorities.

In Dundee this sense of unreality would continue well into the war as the Corporation fought tooth and nail to retain what it saw as democratic control over Civil Defence but, as the orders for the immobilisation of Dundee Harbour show, there was no requirement on those carrying that out even to inform the Corporation of what was being done.

In 1939 the Government, unwilling to trust the local authorities to effectively handle either Civil Defence or the results of air raids, instituted a system of Regional and District Commissioners with the power to take control during an emergency. There was also a belief that air raids would cause widespread panic among the poorer or 'evacuable classes', and it was decided that a sizeable element of the Territorial Army would be kept at home, as one senior officer put it, in order to 'keep the peace . . . and restore law and order in air raids'. Though not made public at the time, Camperdown Estate was

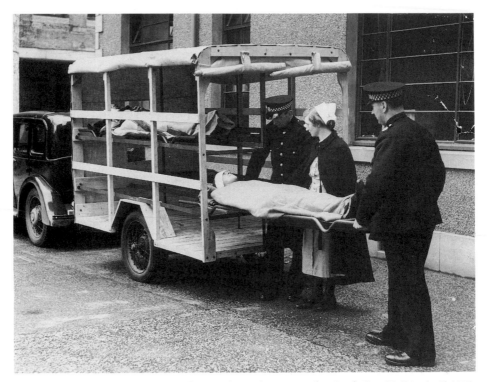

A locally built lightweight trailer ambulance being demonstrated at Perth City Hall in April 1939.
DUNDEE COURIER AND EVENING TELEGRAPH

reserved for use as a 'Military Reinforcement Camp', and Committee Room 3 in the City Chambers as 'Military Operational Control'.

Despite the rising tension in Europe as Hitler threatened Czechoslovakia, during the summer of 1938 the ARP Committee continued to achieve little or nothing. In July, and with the Munich crisis only six weeks away, only 47 wardens had been trained out of the total of 800 required, and it was clear that not only had the ARP issue become embroiled in party politics, but it had also become an administrative nightmare. Virtually all of the Corporation's committees had some say in the matter. The inevitable result was that nothing was being achieved. In September, and under pressure from the Home Office, an Emergency Committee was convened and given both the remit and the necessary powers to clear up the mess.

For the public, the first indication of action being taken came at three p.m. on Friday, 26 August 1938, when the factory hooters, or 'bummers', were sounded in the Hawkhill and Perth Road areas to assess their suitability as air raid sirens, thus, it was hoped, saving the Corporation from having to buy the real thing. They turned out to be virtually inaudible half a mile away and therefore quite useless. After considering this for almost six months, six 4hp Gent sirens were bought, but even these were far from sufficient to provide adequate coverage of the city which was not achieved until early 1941. When the first real alert sounded on 20 October 1939 many were unable to hear it, and areas such as the Hawkhill were still dependent on the blowing of policemen's whistles to signify an alert during the second Clydeside blitz in May 1941.

In the final months of peace there was no more reason to suppose that Dundee would escape massive early attacks by the Luftwaffe than anywhere else, and yet it was in the field of air raid shelters that the record of the city was poorest. Civic parsimony combined with sectional interest to ensure that the city entered the war without one properly completed public shelter in the city centre. The first contracts for the strengthening of nine basements were not issued until the week before war broke out, and by the end of September 1939 the city was only able to boast public shelter accommodation for around 4,000 people, much of which was, in any case, sub-standard or unfinished.

As late as July 1940, with Hitler in Paris for over a month, the city was a long way short of having adequate shelter provision, and yet work was still proceeding on the building of the housing schemes at Kirkton, Beechwood and Polepark. At a meeting of industrial firms held under the aegis of the Chamber of Commerce on 3 July 1940, Captain H. E. Sanderson, the Regional Officer for the Ministry of Home Security, described the position in Dundee as regards civil defence services as 'extremely serious'. Two weeks later, Barclay Brown was writing to David Latto effectively washing the Ministry's hands of the whole affair.

The row finally became a crisis in February 1941 when Ellen Wilkinson, the fiery Labour MP and Under Secretary of State at the Home Office, visited the city. Eighteen months later, Lord Provost Garnet Wilson was still moved to describe the tone of their discussion that day as 'caustic' due to 'our shelter provision not being as efficient as your practical mind demanded'. She had seen the trench shelters at Blue Mountains snow-bound with no attempt being made to clear them, as well as basement shelters with live gas pipes running through them, and had been shown wholly impractical plans for 12 deep tunnel shelters in various points throughout the city. She

Sergeant, later Lieutenant, Robert Brown instructs Constable Richard Louden, Sergeant James Henderson and an unidentified inspector in the workings of the service respirator.
TAYSIDE POLICE MUSEUM

was not to return until August 1943, by which time the situation had been rectified, although the danger had long since passed.

To assume that this inactivity was entirely due to the parsimony and political in-fighting of sections of the Corporation would however be quite unfair. The Ratepayers Association protested loud and long about the 6d (2 ½ p) increase in the rates needed to finance even the most modest effort being made.

The Civil Defence Act of 1939 required employers with more than 50 employees to provide shelters within their premises along with wardens trained by the Corporation ARP Department. Reluctant to pay even the small fee sought for this service by the Corporation, they were quick to ensure they would be compensated at the full rate of 10/- (50p) for men and 7/- (35p) for women per day should their trained wardens be needed by the city's ARP service.

In addition, the Corporation were receiving mixed messages from the Government on the level of urgency required. A week after the crisis over Czechoslovakia began, they were being told that there was 'a need for urgent action', and yet, a mere two weeks later, they were told that 'ARP should be carried on in a more leisurely manner'. In April 1939 they received a Government request to accelerate Civil Defence work at the expense of other business, despite which they were being constantly pressured over the amount of corrugated iron and wood being used. Given the fact that ARP had by then become a political football in Dundee, this official dithering only served to ensure that nothing was done.

When gauging public reaction to this lack of preparation it is important to remember that, pre-war, there was little public understanding of what was meant by Air Raid Precautions. It was not until the war was well under way that the full extent of the measures required became widely known. In December 1940 one petition demanding adequate shelter provision was supported by over 8,000 signatures. This growing public disquiet was fuelled by a sustained campaign of criticism in the columns of the D. C. Thomson papers. On 19 November 1940, in one of its more memorable leaders on the subject and under a headline, 'Some questions which have reached us', the *Courier* asked:

> What is Dundee Town Council waiting for?
> Why do the anti-aircraft guns not shoot the raiders down?
> Who gives the directions for sounding sirens?
> What is the Rotary Club doing about it?
> Why do the searchlights shine on the city?
> Why doesn't our Town Council get busy like the Town Councils of Glasgow and Aberdeen?
> Why searchlights, shelters and no shooting?
> What is the Business Club doing about it?

Ten days later further questions asked in a leader page included:

> Why searchlights, bombs and then sirens?
> Why should searchlights be allowed to spoil the blackout?
> What is a Town Councillor for?
> Is it possible that someone in authority has sung an official lullaby and sent the Town Council away to dreamland?
> Why is there so much secrecy about municipal affairs?
> What are 330,000 German soldiers in Norway for?

On 18 August 1939, just over two weeks before the start of hostilities and when all but the most determined optimist would have seen war as at least highly likely, the question of whether a range of protective measures should be undertaken at the city's hospitals was deferred for consideration of likely cost.

When the ARP Controller was quietly replaced in October 1939 by Councillor William Hughes, who was to serve with distinction in that role until 1943, the Corporation thanked the previous incumbent, and by definition itself, for 'his efforts to ensure the city was in a satisfactory state of preparedness on the outbreak of war'.

The Means of Protection – Civil Defence

Now it came to pass in the year of the World War that an host assembled at a place called the yaird.

And the leader of the host was one Philip, one skilful in the drawing of plans.

And Philip said unto them, 'We will even show unto them all manner of men the manner in which to quench flames with our stiripump.'

Anon. From the Harbour ARP Organisation.

On the evening of 26 September 1938 Adolf Hitler told an enthusiastic crowd in the Berlin Sportspalast that the Sudetenland would be in German hands by 'peace or war' on 1 October. The following morning trench shelters were being dug in Dundee's parks.

In the 1930s it was the accepted wisdom that war on the civilian population would take two forms: the dropping of high explosive and incendiary bombs, and the spreading of poison gas. To meet this double threat two forms of protection would be needed: hardened shelters and the whole paraphernalia of anti-gas warfare, both of which would require to be co-ordinated by a report and control network and provided with a range of support services.

The most urgent need, in Dundee as elsewhere, was for trained personnel and early in 1938 it had been estimated that 3,851 men and women would be required, a hard core of whom would be paid staff supported by a massive voluntary effort. On the night of 27 September, public meetings were held in the Caird Hall and the YMCA in Broughty Ferry at which the city started to recruit the first of the 800 air raid wardens required.

During Exercise 'Rabbit' in August 1941, men of the Auxiliary Fire Service demonstrate a particularly uncomfortable procedure for removing a casualty from a bombed-out house – in reality, the rear of 30 Noran Avenue, Craigiebank.

Detective Constable Peter Fletcher, fresh from his involvement in the Jordan affair, was appointed Robert Brown's assistant and sent to the Government Anti Gas School at Easingwold. He returned at the end of September with a First Class Instructor's (Special) Certificate, and Brown was able to inform the Corporation that the training programme would start in mid-October. At first, temporary premises in the City Chambers had to be used while a search for permanent accommodation for the ARP Training Centre went on.

For wardens, the training consisted of 22 hours spent on anti-gas warfare, six hours on protection against high explosive bombs and eight hours on firefighting and incendiary bomb control. It also included dealing with hazardous chemicals, the recognition of unexploded bombs and incident reporting. The course lasted for a week at the end of which the trainees were required to sit an exam which, should they pass it, qualified them to act as local ARP instructors training further wardens within their sector or factory.

In the Spring of 1939 a permanent home for the ARP Training Centre was found in the former Deaf and Dumb Institute in Dudhope Terrace Road which had four lecture rooms and a gas chamber in the basement. Another gas chamber had been constructed in the loft of the Police Headquarters in Bell Street but this was small and difficult to get to. With the approach of war, the warden service would be responsible for fitting 180,000 gas masks to the entire civilian population of the city, and it was in these two chambers that, coughing and weeping in billowing clouds of tear gas, they were trained for this task.

Whilst almost all saw this training as necessary, some were not quite so convinced. During the summer of 1939, as schools were seen as particularly vulnerable, the Education Committee arranged for ARP training for groups of teachers. Some of the teachers took a dim view of having to give up things such as golf tournaments and expressed their unhappiness in a lively exchange of views with Peter Fletcher. Having behaved in a manner that would have done credit to the most rowdy of children, one future headmaster complained to members of the Education Committee, and is understood to have received some well chosen words of advice from Garnet Wilson, then Education Convener, and Councillor Lily Miller.

Training was not confined to Civil Defence personnel; nurses were being shown how best to protect the elderly and disabled, and how to fit infants' gas masks. At Lawside Convent, the nuns were being shown how to fight fires with a stirrup pump and, on Sunday nights, the city's halls and cinemas were used for public meetings when films on poison gas and fire fighting would be shown.

Again in Noran Avenue, this time outside No. 45, a warden acts as a 'casualty' for a first-aid party. The stretcher bearers are carrying heavy-duty service respirators on their chests and their first-aid kits over their shoulders. The party leader is denoted by his white helmet. The calm, ordered, even non-chalant atmosphere, typified by the cigarette-smoking stretcher bearer with his helmet pushed back, is in stark contrast to the grimmer realities experienced by the victims of heavy bombing.

Even the serious nature of the subject could not dim the Dundee sense of humour; on one occasion an instructor at a public meeting was told that he should 'nip into the kitchen' as the woman making the tea was 'a sure thing'! On another, having just shown a film to a group of trainee wardens, an instructor turned to his audience and said 'Well, Ladies and Gentlemen, you have all seen that if an incendiary bomb comes through your ceiling, don't lose your head—put it in a bucket and cover it with sand.'

At last, and amid clear signs of a more dynamic approach to ARP, in April 1939 Robert Brown was able to report that 620 wardens had received anti-gas training and that a further 293 were under training.

A fire-fighting demonstration in City Square, with two wardens about to operate a hand stirrup pump. In the foreground are a sand bucket and scoop used for dealing with small incendiaries.
FROM THE COLLECTION OF PETER FLETCHER

Rescue Squads were the responsibility of the City Engineer's Department and had their own training school at the Corporation Depot in Foundry Lane. Here they learned the difficult and dangerous art of extracting people from collapsed buildings. At Fairfield Depot squads were being trained in the decontamination of buildings, food and clothing which had been affected by poison gas. Demolition Squads and Repair Parties were being formed and large numbers of vehicles made available for the removal of rubble. Ambulance drivers were being trained in how to drive safely over broken glass and, inevitably, a battalion of administrators was forming up. In addition, older organisations such as the Red Cross were seeking members, and a number of new organisations such as the Women's Auxiliary Police Corps and the Womens Voluntary Service were being formed.

Having been trained, this civilian army needed equipment and thousands of uniforms, stirrup pumps, buckets and sand scoops for dealing with incendiaries were bought. One order in 1939 included over 400 first aid outfits and handbells, 800 notebooks and gas warning rattles, and 1,200 whistles and torches. Even ministers were to be issued with steel helmets and armbands to allow them to move around in air raids and give comfort to victims. A meeting of Dundee Presbytery in September 1939 was pleased to note that steel helmets at 8/6d (42½p) were somewhat cheaper than standard clerical headgear.

Casualty figures from Zeppelin raids on London during the First World War were extrapolated to give estimates of those that could be expected in a new conflict. In Dundee it was decided that 164 casualty vehicles would be required for air raid duty. Included in this total were 90 ambulances, 60 cars for sitting cases and seven converted buses, all of which would be stationed at six depots throughout the city, along with as many as 92 personnel at each depot during an alert. When war broke out there were five ambulances in Dundee, though 140 casualty vehicles were available by 1942.

Further, thought was given to the city's pre-war mortuary provision which was sufficient for 44 bodies. As this was deemed inadequate Balgray Farm was requisitioned and converted at a cost of over £2,000 to increase capacity to 350, and 12 Union Jacks were bought for use as palls. Should the city's own casualty services be unable to cope with the transport of corpses, the Government would pay the owners of private vehicles 5/- (25p) per hour plus 1/6d (7½p) per body, or 10/-(50p) per full load to undertake the task. Petrol was to be supplied by the Corporation.

By 1940 the Casualty Services had set up First Aid Posts at a number of locations, including the Eastern School, Ancrum Road School, Dens Road School and Sharps Mill in Blinshall Street. Some enterprising citizens were also setting up their own First Aid Posts, including one in an old van body in the front garden of 9 Abbotsford Place. Gas Decontamination Centres were established at Constable Street Baths, Maryfield Hospital and Ashludie Sanatorium, along with Emergency Medical Service Hospitals at Dundee Royal Infirmary, Maryfield Hospital, Fernbrae Nursing Home and Elliot Road Nursing Home.

One result of widespread bombing would have been a large number of people made homeless, and the Emergency Relief Organisation, equipped with hundreds of camp beds, dozens of cots and thousands of blankets, was hastily set up to deal with that eventuality. In December 1941 it was reported that Rest Centres for air raid victims at the Palais Dance Hall in South Tay Street, Morgan Academy, Kidd's Rooms, Downfield Masonic Hall in Duncan Street and 48 other locations could provide accommodation for 8,684 people, and that 2,000 volunteers were available to assist. Despite the optimistic assessment, closer examination based on experience gained during the London blitz revealed that, amongst other things, arrangements for catering and sanitation were wholly inadequate. This led to the summary dismissal of the Emergency Relief Officer though the real blame for the deficiencies lay with the Government, which had refused to provide some of the requirements on the basis that doing so would encourage people of the so-called poorer classes to stay in Rest Centres.

Another consequence of heavy raids would have been a breakdown in food distribution and, centred on the Dundee Food Office in the Overgate, a large number of food stores were set up throughout the city. Arrangements were also made for the mass feeding of the population from kitchens set up on, for example, Caird Park Golf Course and Fountainbleau Drive.

In 1939, despite pre-war efforts at rationalisation, there were still 1,688 entirely separate fire forces in Britain. In addition to these there existed the new Auxiliary Fire Service made up largely of volunteers manning trailer pumps. This recipe for chaos, which would not be resolved until 1941 with the formation of a unified National Fire Service, would result in situations such as that where, during the 1940 blitz on Coventry, the neighbouring Birmingham Fire Brigade was unable to help as its fittings were of a different size. As late as 1942 many of the works hydrants in Dundee were still not compatible with the fittings used by the National Fire Service.

The Control Room of 'A' division of the No. 4 (Eastern) Fire Force Area was in 17 Union Street, Dundee and sub-divisions covered the city centre, the northern part of the city and Broughty Ferry. Within the three divisions there were 23 fire stations in 1942 in addition to the three which had existed pre-war. These included Crawford Lodge on the Perth Road, the Heinz Building at Carolina Port, Cosgrove's Garage in Kincardine Street, Downfield School, the Armitstead Home and Dens Works.

As the ARP Training Centre in Dudhope Park was turning out trained personnel, others were concerned with the setting up of the Report and Control System within which they would operate. The city was split into four divisions, the first being Broughty Ferry with 12,000 inhabitants. Each division had its own Report and Control Centre and in Broughty Ferry this was in the former Municipal Buildings.

The Eastern Division contained 53,750 residents along with Carolina Port Power Station, the Gas Works and the Harbour. Here, the Divisional Report and Control Centre was established in the gymnasium at Victoria Road School, Craigiebank Church Hall was designated a Rest Centre for air raid victims, and ARP Personnel Depots were set up at Foundry Lane and Craigie Quarry in Rodd Road. Each division also had an ARP administrative headquarters, in this case at 1 Victoria Road.

50,500 people lived in the Western Division, prime targets here being the Police and Fire Headquarters, the Telephone Exchange, the Transport Department and many industrial premises. Divisional Control, after a short period in City Square, moved to the basement of Friarfield House in Barrack Street, a Rest Centre was established at Logie School on Blackness Road and Personnel Depots were next to St John's Cross Church on Blackness Avenue and at the Corporation Depot in Miln Street. The Wardens Divisional Headquarters was at 48 South Tay Street. In May 1941, a decoy fire site was established on Riverside Drive which was designed to tempt enemy bombers away from real targets within the city.

The largely residential Northern Division, which included Lochee, had Rest Centres in Clepington School in Sandeman Street and Lawside Academy in Lawside Road, a Personnel Depot in Fairfield Street Yard and its Divisional Headquarters in a hut at the corner of Russell Street and Strathmartine Road. In 1939 the former tenants of the garden ground on which this hut was being built claimed, and were given, £3 each for 'loss of plants'. The Report and Control Centre was in the basement of Coldside Library which was specially strengthened for the purpose. Here, during an alert, there were to be as many as 18 working in the Control Room and another nine in the Message Room in addition to five messengers.

Whilst each division had considerable autonomy in dealing with incidents in its own area, they were in turn responsible to a main Report and Control Centre which was initially set up in 14 City Square. Arrangements here were somewhat haphazard and by 1941 this had moved to a purpose-built bunker in the front garden at 7 Scotswood Terrace where the house was also taken over to provide accommodation. This Central Control was manned during an alert by the Medical Officer of Health as Head of Casualty Services, the City Engineer as Head of Rescue Services, the Head of Decontamination Services from the Cleansing Department, the Senior Gas Identification Officer, representatives from the Gas, Water and Electricity Departments, Reinforcement Officers, the Emergency Relief Officer and the First Aid

During Exercise Jute in June 1942, a bowler-hatted Major Barclay Brown confers with Peter Fletcher in Park Place, Dundee. Fletcher is carrying the Leica camera with which he took a number of the photographs included in this book.
FROM THE COLLECTION OF PETER FLETCHER

Buildings Repairs Officer. In charge of operations were ARP Controller Councillor William Hughes, Robert Brown or Peter Fletcher as ARP Officers, and Hugh Mill as Chief Warden.

As the city's largest public utility, the Harbour Trust were required to provide their own ARP organisation, the surviving records of which provide a graphic account of the difficulties and frustrations experienced by those charged with running such a service.

In 1940 the Harbour ARP organisation still had no official standing within the city's main ARP organisation with the absurd result that they were not officially being given information on vitally important matters such as the latest types of bombs being used by the enemy. They were also finding it extremely difficult to recruit volunteer wardens. As late as February 1941 not one permanent docker was prepared to volunteer, and dock gatemen were refusing to answer appeals to man their posts during an air raid alert. On the Friday evening before a major Civil Defence exercise later that year, a public demonstration of the equipment in the Report Centre was arranged for which nobody turned up.

Even those few prepared to undertake the punishing rota of duty in the Harbour Report Centre in addition to their full-time occupations found themselves subject to pre-war levels of bureaucracy. One memo complained about the fact that four dozen pencils had been issued to the Report Centre in four months, stating that 'in future staff will use their own pencils unless during operations. Pencils for operational use will be kept locked up in the locker above the field telephone.'

Training was often sketchy and, in 1942, the Officer in Charge of the Harbour Report Centre was moved to comment that the 'standard of training of those on night duty at the Harbour is very, very low'. Further, some of the training that was done was based on wildly inaccurate assessments of the enemy's ingenuity. On Sunday, 22 September 1940, wardens posts in the city were told that reports had been received of material like cobwebs being dropped from enemy aircraft which, in one case, was said to have caused blistering when touched. This turned out to be nothing more harmful than gossamer discharged by spiders while mating in mid-air. Three days later, Gas Identification Officers and other personnel were scouring fields north of the city after reports that similar material had been seen falling from a passing enemy bomber.

That disillusionment and disagreements were an almost daily feature of life in the ARP service is hardly surprising given the treatment of staff and volunteers. Less than a month after the outbreak of war, in an ill-considered overreaction of gossip about supposedly wealthy full-time wardens taking wages they did not need, the Corporation announced that it was going to means test all paid ARP staff. This was in spite of the fact that desperately low wages of between £1-10/- (£1.50) and £2 for women and £2-10/- (£2.50) and £3 for men per week were hardly of the order that would attract war profiteers.

Embarrassingly, it was later reported that, following an investigation, three women had voluntarily returned £2 and one man had given back 10/- (50p). It was even necessary for the minister of St Luke's church in Lochee to announce from the pulpit that his work with the first aid post in Ancrum Road was entirely unpaid.

A first-aid party deal with a 'casualty' in Whorterbank, Lochee, during an exercise in June 1942.
DUNDEE COURIER AND EVENING TELEGRAPH

Further controversy arose that autumn when the cost of providing food for voluntary ARP staff on night duty became the subject of heated debate in the Corporation chamber. With scarcely concealed glee, the *People's Journal* reported that some workers were indignant at the suggestion that they were 'guzzling tons of money' when they had 'never seen a bridie'!

By December 1939 the massive air attack that was feared had failed to materialise and, as a cost cutting exercise, the Government decided to reduce the size of the ARP services. In Dundee the number of paid staff was to be cut from 322 to 250 and it was decided that the simplest way to achieve this would be to dismiss all 68 paid female wardens. One Baillie thought that this was the best way out of an embarrassing situation and said that 'it was better to dispense with all the women than attempt to make a selection'. Lamely, Robert Brown added that he hoped they would all continue to serve on a voluntary basis and, to their credit, a great many of them did just that. One memorable letter which appeared in the *People's Journal* at this time stated that, despite the need for increased war production, 'women should be kept out of men's jobs'.

A further crisis arose late in July 1940 when 20 volunteer wardens at the Rockwell School post resigned *en masse*. This followed similar resignations from the post in Hill Street as a protest at the condition of the posts which were three-sided playsheds, the fourth side having been made up with sandbags. These sandbags, in place by then for almost a year, had largely rotted away leaving the posts open to the weather and unable to be lit owing to blackout restrictions. In the ensuing confrontation the Corporation was threatened with further resignations and was forced into an ignominious climb down. Within a week, work was under way to bring the posts up to an acceptable standard, and a paid warden who had been sacked for daring to protest at the state of the post in Hill Street had been reinstated.

In September 1941, all the various ARP and fire services were brought together under the collective title of Civil Defence. In October the following year it was decided that women aged between 20 and 45 should be called up as Firewatchers. What followed remains as an excellent example of the muddled arrangements the public endured during the war. On the day of registration, women, many with small children, stood for hours from early morning in a queue which stretched the length of Gellatly Street. Amid mounting chaos the registration carried on into the following week with around 1,000 women laying siege to the Fire Guard Office at the bottom of the Hilltown every day. The waste of time and effort involved is well illustrated by the fact that, owing to conflicting commitments to other services, many thousands of those so laboriously registered were in any case exempt.

For those involved, Civil Defence represented a considerable commitment of free time. In addition to volunteer warden or firewatching duties there were regular exercises lasting up to 24 hours over the weekend, as often as once a month. Boredom was, however, a feature of long nights spent on duty, and a new social structure was created around the ARP organisation as wardens' posts and Auxiliary Fire Stations challenged each other to table tennis matches or quizzes, and dances or social evenings were held.

Exercises and public demonstrations also provided their own brand of light relief. One public demonstration given by the Auxiliary Fire Service at Fairfield Depot resulted in them setting fire to their own appliance and having to send for another to put it out!

A major gas exercise was held in the city centre on the afternoon of Thursday, 24 April 1941, during which canisters of tear gas were released at various points resulting in the High Street, Reform Street and the Wellgate literally disappearing under a white noxious cloud within which locals and visitors alike were expected to carry on as normal while wearing their gas masks. One Deputy Chief Warden who is remembered as being 'a bit interfering' had been annoying ARP Department staff conducting the exercise and it was decided that something would have to be done. A small quantity of gas crystals was placed alongside the manifold of his car before he drove off and, as one of those present put it, 'there was no more trouble with him'! Dr Robert Roger, a lecturer in Chemistry at University College Dundee who specialised in dealing with the effects of gas warfare, decided to enliven proceedings during this exercise by testing one of his own concoctions. This he did by throwing a capsule of the stuff which, though harmless, is remembered as absolutely horrible, down the steps of the Westport public toilet, to the considerable discomfort of the occupants!

Dr Roger also has the distinction of very nearly burning down a large part of the University. One Saturday afternoon, and after some time of asking, Peter Fletcher was able to provide him with an incendiary bomb to examine. Joining Roger in his laboratory, Fletcher watched with mounting alarm as he first clamped the bomb in a vice and then set about removing the contents with the end of a file. Inevitably, the bomb went off, setting fire to lab coats hanging on the wall and sending both Fletcher and Roger scurrying for extinguishers.

In the more selfish society of over half a century later it is hard to grasp the magnitude of the operation that the Civil Defence Services became when they reached their peak in Dundee early in 1942. At the end of the war, the Corporation was attempting to secure the return of around 9,000 steel helmets that had been issued over the preceding six years.

Perhaps the last word on the Civil Defence Services should come from an anonymous Fire Guard writing as the service was disbanded in late 1944;

The Dundee Firewatcher's Farewell

Fareweel tae sleeping bag and bed
Whaur near the flair we laid oor head.
Fareweel tae auld grey army blankit
For that an' mair the Lord be thankit.

Nae mair o' 'gutsy' darts or nap
For noo we're on the war's last lap.
Nae listenin' tae the siren's warnin'
Nae creepin' hame on a wintry mornin'.

Nae signin' on nor signin' aff,
We'll miss oor pal's good natured chaff.
For noo we'll lead a sheltered life,
Nae lees about duty tae the wife.

Nae mair three bobs—they were sae handy
For "nippin" up the road tae see "Andy".
Oor duty's done—but lads it's tame
Tae sit and watch the fire—at hame.

The Means of Protection – Air Raid Shelters

One of the enduring images of the Second World War is of air raid shelters filled with people singing the songs of Harry Lauder or Vera Lynn and generally keeping their chins up. The reality of shelter life was a long way removed from the myth; it was damp, dark, bitterly cold, often verminous and insanitary, and usually boring. In addition there was always the thought that this time 'it might just be aimed at me'.

It was in the area of shelter provision that Dundee lagged most seriously behind the rest of the country. There were three different types of shelter provision in the city: public shelters for those caught in the open during a raid at, for example, the bus stance in Shore Terrace, communal domestic shelters such as those built in the street outside tenements; and ordinary domestic shelters, the most common of which was the Anderson Shelter. In addition there were shelters provided for the specific needs of groups such as factory workers and school children.

First to appear were trench shelters dug on open ground at, for example, the corner of Provost Road and Dens Road. These were six feet deep with the sides revetted with corrugated iron and covered over with corrugated iron and turf. Basement shelters were constructed in strong buildings selected by the City Engineer. They were strengthened with steel beams and concrete and access doors were protected with sandbags. A small number of closes were designated as shelters after being protected with blast walls at either end. These were quite useless and all but abandoned by 1941.

Whilst the brick and concrete surface shelters so redolent of the period did not begin to appear in any number until early 1940, the most common shelter of all appeared in 1939. Anderson shelters, named after the then Lord Privy Seal Sir John Anderson, were issued free to households with annual incomes of less than £250, otherwise costing £8 each. Provided as a self-assembly kit of sheets of corrugated iron, it was this that was to gain them some notoriety in Dundee. By January 1940 only 25% of the 3,131 Anderson shelters delivered in Dundee had been built, and during that winter the city's children discovered that sections of Anderson shelter made excellent sledges and helter skelters. As a result, the Chief Constable was instructed to prosecute offenders for misuse of Government property. As late as December 1941 the Ministry of Home Security were threatening to remove Anderson shelters not properly constructed from Dundee to other cities where they felt they would be appreciated.

Another type of domestic shelter which saw limited use in the city was the Morrison shelter. It was a steel-framed cage designed to take the place of a kitchen table and was just big enough for a family to crawl inside.

At the outbreak of war the Emergency Committeee asked the LMS Railway Company for the use of the Law Tunnel as a shelter. This was agreed to at a rent of £1 per annum, provided the Corporation undertook to return the tunnel to the condition in which they found it. In February 1941, Ellen Wilkinson noted that Law Tunnel had no amenities and described it as one of the wettest shelters she had ever seen. In addition it was extremely cold and was never a success. Plans for a grid square of tunnels westwards of the present tunnel with exits to Kinghorne Road were quietly dropped.

Amongst the 12 other locations being surveyed for deep tunnels in 1940 were Windsor Street, Seabraes, Parker Street, Dens Brae, South Baffin Street, Dalgleish Road and Whinny Brae. This wholly impractical scheme was based on the spurious assertion that the citizens of Birmingham had been provided with deep shelters at Government expense. The tunnels, which were to have provided dormitory accommodation for around 5,000 people would have taken years to construct and would have cost an enormous sum at a time when the real need was for the accelerated building of surface shelters. At no time was it made clear on what basis the said 5,000 people were to be selected. A similar scheme was considered by Glasgow Corporation though never seriously.

While most owners of property required for the building of shelters gave it up without demur and free of charge for the duration, others were not so

Caird Avenue in June 1942 and a head warden is giving instructions to one of the 52 boys recruited for the Police Auxiliary Messenger Service. Often these messages were of a wholly domestic nature and were delivered to homes rather than civil defence or military headquarters.

DUNDEE COURIER AND EVENING TELEGRAPH

public spirited. Some property companies sought to charge rent and others, including Lord Provost Phin's ironmongery business, made claims for disturbance payments. The owners of the King's Theatre would only grant the use of their basement as a shelter after they had received a written undertaking from the Corporation stating that they would return it to its former condition after the war.

In April 1941 an inspection of the shelters in the city centre revealed basement shelters in Gellatly Street which flooded with every high tide and four shelters which used open braziers for heating. It was noted that there was 'a good deal of misuse of shelters not provided with doors'. A wider survey that July found that only five per cent of shelters were heated and that 20% failed to comply with minimum ventilation standards. Further, it was noted that almost 50% of communal domestic shelters were dirty and that a large number were infested with bugs, rats and beetles. There were also complaints that the shelters at Mitchell Street School were difficult to get to owing to 'goats in the vicinity'. This report was described by the Regional Commissioner for Scotland, Lord Rosebery, as 'very unsatisfactory'.

The first positive report on the city's shelters does not appear until 4 September 1941, when the Regional Shelters Officer was pleased to note that 'a great deal had been done since Miss Wilkinson's visit last February'. He continued, stating that 'A great amount of work still requires to be done, but Dundee is doing as well as any other town in Scotland at present'. He made favourable comment on the fact that by then 75% of shelters had been provided with seats, that 80% had a drinking water supply and that all but 40 basement shelters were electrically lit. Only at this time was he able to report that there were no live gas pipes in basement shelters ready to incinerate anyone unwise enough use them.

Not all shelters were built to the standards required by the Ministry of Home Security. By September 1941, 43 shelters in the city had been replaced due to shoddy workmanship. In August 1942 David and Millar Thomson, partners in the building firm of D.&W. Thomson, 234 Queen Street, Broughty Ferry, were both sentenced to two years hard labour when it was discovered that eight shelters they had built at the Eastern School and Grove Academy were seriously sub-standard. Instead of having solid brick walls, those at the Eastern School had been constructed using single brick cavity walls filled with loose rubble and sand. Questions were asked as to why this had not been noticed by the Corporation's Clerk of Works. He was able to point out that he had not been able to visit the site as often as he would have liked, as complaints made by both elected members and the D. C. Thomson newspapers about his supposedly excessive use of Corporation cars had led to his being forced to use the restricted wartime public transport service.

By the end of 1941 the city was able to boast a total of 9,588 shelters of various types with accommodation for a total of 144,471 people. Included in this total were 136 trenches, 267 basements, 2,049 surface shelters and 6,560 Anderson shelters. Not until the end of May 1942, almost three years into the war, would Garnet Wilson be able to write to Ellen Wilkinson saying that, with regard to shelters, Dundee was 'well nigh leading the country in its progress' and that 'she might like to escape the critical atmosphere of the House of Commons and make a return visit'.

Chapter Four

'Demolition Charges have been Prepared'

(STANDING OPERATIONAL INSTRUCTIONS –
ANGUS SUB-AREA COMMAND, 1941)

On 4 October 1938 Dundee Corporation agreed to lease a 7.36-acre site at Douglas Wood near Wellbank to the Air Ministry for an unspecified use. In agreeing the lease, the Corporation, bureaucratic to the last, insisted on an undertaking that the ground was 'not required for camping purposes and that no habitations are to be erected in the area' and, further, that their tenant at Downiebank Farm should have access to the site to water his stock. By the following Spring the tall lattice work masts of RAF Douglas Wood Chain Home RDF Station dominated the skyline and the site had become one of the most secret in the country.

Chain Home was the primitive form of radar hurriedly installed around that time to supplement the network of Observer Corps posts, radio listening posts and other intelligence gathering services which formed the command and control network used by the RAF during the Battle of Britain in 1940. Contrary to the myths that have grown up about the part played by radar at the time, Chain Home had a 300% factor of inaccuracy and was largely useless below 5,000 feet. A new system called Chain Home Low was devised in response to this last problem and a station set up at St Cyrus near Montrose.

Initially, the Dundee, Angus and north Fife area fell within 13 Group Fighter Command, and defensive deployments of operational units to RAF Montrose and RAF Leuchars took place on the outbreak of war. During the Battle of Britain a number of units badly mauled during the fall of France and in the actions which followed over the Channel were sent north to rest and reform. At Montrose these included the Spitfires of B Flight 603 Squadron, Hurricanes from 111 Squadron, Defiants of 141 Squadron and, at Leuchars in late 1940, the Spitfires of 65 and 72 Squadrons.

The issue of coastal defences became urgent following the disasters in Norway and France. Royal Observer Corps Posts had been set up at Scotscraig by Tayport and at Magdalene's, Kirkton in Dundee. By June 1940 6″ naval gun batteries had been built at St Andrews and on the shore just to the east of the Caledon Shipyard, and three torpedo tubes manned by ratings from HMS *Ambrose*, the naval shore establishment in Dundee, had been installed on the Eastern Wharf. Road blocks and machine gun posts had been established on the Caledon Bridge, at the Camperdown Gate and at the Custom House manned by seamen from HMS *Unicorn* and army personnel. Tank traps and trenches were dug and the first of thousands of mines were being laid along the coast. A range of vulnerable points in and around the city were identified, including the Port War Signal Station at Buddon Ness, The Post Office Garage in Trades Lane, Briggs Oil Refinery and the Tay Bridge. During the height of the invasion scare in 1940 the Tay Bridge (VP 235) was guarded by the 9th Battalion Black Watch.

In July, controlled minefields were being installed at sea off Buddon Ness and Broughty Castle. At Broughty Ferry this ingenious weapon consisted of 12 mines in four groups of three held at a fixed depth under water which could be fired from a position on the roof of the castle should any unwelcome visitors try to enter the river. Also at the castle, two 6″ guns were installed in the Castle Green Battery during April 1940 followed by a 4.7″ battery for 'local protection and emergency use', and the castle became the headquarters of 503 Coast Regiment Royal Artillery, guarded by two platoons of C Company 2nd Battalion City of Dundee Home Guard. By 1942 the batteries between Montrose and Stannergate, Dundee, had come under the control of the 13 officers and 350 men of 543 Coast Regiment Royal Artillery, and regular firing practices were being held to seaward. In May 1942 following the reduction in the threat of invasion, the coastal artillery establishment was considerably reduced.

In early 1941 417 Searchlight Battery Royal Artillery was based at Dryburgh Farm and nearby Lansdowne House with 24 detachments within an area to the north of the city bounded by Errol, Newtyle, Glamis, Carmyllie and Arbroath. 93 Bomb Disposal Unit Royal Engineers was operating from 'Foxmount', Reres Road, Broughty Ferry, and Balgowan School was being turned into a Military Detention Barracks or, as it was more commonly known, the 'Glasshouse'.

By 1943 Dryburgh Farm had become the headquarters of 147 Heavy Anti-Aircraft Regiment Royal Artillery which had troops based at Strathmore Avenue, Kingsway West, Stannergate, and included Polish batteries based at Longtown Crescent, Mid Craigie and at RAF Douglas Wood. 5 Maritime

On Wednesday, 11 December 1940 Lieutenant General Sir Alan Brooke, accompanied by General Sikorski, G.O.C. Polish Forces, and General Carrington, C. in C. Scottish Command, undertook an inspection of Polish Forces defending the Angus coastline. This four-inch gun emplacement was at Carnoustie.

Detachment, Maritime Anti-Aircraft Regiment, Royal Artillery, was headquartered at 7 Lynnewood Place off Madiera Street, Dundee, and ammunition distribution points had been identified at Glamis and at Muirhead School. In the event of an invasion, communications with the Muirhead School ammunition point would have relied on the telephone in the nearby manse.

Responsibility for the defence of the Angus coastline largely rested with units of the Polish Army which had re-formed in exile in Scotland during 1940. With the Angus Sub-area Headquarters at Hillbank, Forfar, the 5th Cadre Brigade were based at Broughty Ferry, the 7th at Brechin and the 3rd at Buddon with one unit detached to Arbroath. Also based in the Forfar area were the Infantry Battalion of the 1st Anti Tank Regiment and the 10th Mechanised Cavalry Regiment.

As the harbours at Dundee, Montrose and Arbroath would clearly be of considerable value to an invader, orders were drawn up for their immobilisation.

Secret

On receipt of the selected code word the DUNDEE Harbour Trust will take the following action:-

a) Place the blockship in Camperdown Basin in the arranged position at the dock entrance. The ship is to be prepared for sinking which however will not be carried out until further orders.

b) Immobilisation of electric and steam cranes in the precincts of the harbour under their control.

c) Assemble all tugs, lighters and steam vessels including the Tay Ferries and prepare to move them to positions to be decided at the time. Preparations also to be made to immobilise these vessels when instructed. These vessels will not actually be immobilised until the very last moment, as they are likely to be required for the movement of troops from the north to the south bank of the River Tay or vice versa.

d) Open the caisson connecting the north and south shores of the cutting between Victoria and Camperdown Docks, and remove the chains to prevent it being reclosed.

e) Order the removal of all rolling stock and particularly locomotives from the precincts of the harbour. Remove vital parts of the sub-station and pumping plants at the West and East Graving Docks.

f) Completion of the above mentioned actions is to be reported to the Naval Officer in Charge, Dundee.

On receipt of the instruction ''Emergency Crane Precautions'' the General Manager of the Caledon Shipbuilding Yard will instruct the following action to be taken:-

a) Immobilise the 130 ton crane at the boiler shop jetty, the crane at the fitting out jetty and all gantry cranes in the precincts of the Caledon Yard.

b) Make preparations to move and, if necessary, sink any vessels alongside their fitting out wharves.

c) Immobilise the firm's power station at the boiler shop entrance.

The Naval Officer in Charge will take the following action:-

a) Report to the Admiralty by means of Most Immediate Secret Signal ''Port of Dundee Immobilising''.

Machine-gun nests were built on the Esplanade at Broughty Ferry against seaborne invasion. Beyond this one, from which Brooke is emerging followed by Sikorski, can be seen concrete 'dragons' teeth' anti-tank defences at the mouth of the Dighty Burn.

b) Arrange for the various prepared demolition charges to be instantly available should demolition be deemed necessary.

c) Decide which ships should be prepared for sinking at the Eastern, King George V and Western Wharves.

d) Inform Captain (S) 9, so that such action as he considers necessary may be taken.

e) Inform the District Commissioner that the port has been immobilised.

f) Report to the Admiralty by means of Most Immediate Secret Signal "Port of Dundee Immobilised".

During the first trial immobilisation, which took place in early April 1941, the Harbour Trust took 14 minutes to complete their part of the operation, both the Navy and the Caledon Yard taking 34 minutes.

Shortly after one a.m. on Monday 13 May 1940 Colonel M.E. Lindsay received the following enquiry from the District Commissioner, Sir John Phin;

> An unconfirmed report received in London says that bands of civilians are forming all over the country and arming themselves with shotguns etc for the purpose of detecting and dealing with German parachutists. Will you please report the position in your district (Fife) to the District Commissioner's office by 0800 hrs on 13th May 1940.

A similar request was sent to Colonel Hew Blair Imrie, Zone Commander for the area north of the Tay, including Dundee. Later that day Colonel Lindsay replied that he was not aware of any such bands of civilians, but at 1820 hours the following day official notification came through of the formation of the Local Defence Volunteers, later rechristened by Churchill the Home Guard.

Within an hour of an appeal broadcast by Anthony Eden, the Secretary of State for War, Alexander Nisbet became the first of hundreds of volunteers drawn from men aged between 17 and 65 not required for military service who were joining up in Dundee, and by noon the following day 259 men had enrolled. By that evening 60 men aged between 19 and 64 had offered their services in Carnoustie along with 94 in Montrose and 200 in Forfar. By 18 May some 1,200 men and women from Dundee and Broughty Ferry had volunteered for duty in what had by then been nicknamed the 'parachute potter-atters'.

These enthusiastic new recruits, with little training or equipment, were required to operate against an enemy fifth column, sabotage and seaborne or airborne landings. To do this they were to help to defend vulnerable points such as factories and public utilities such as water, gas and electricity. They were also to man roadblocks of which there were 33 in Dundee alone, arrange for the defence of towns and villages and deal effectively with an enemy invader 'in whatever guise he might be dressed'. Scares about the enemy using disguise were fuelled by the Dutch Foreign Minister who told an enthralled audience in London of parachutists having landed in his country dressed as tram conductors, Red Cross nurses, nuns and monks! One Dundonian, newly returned from Antwerp, told a clearly awstruck *Courier* reporter sinister tales of women he had seen being arrested as enemy parachutists, saboteurs and spies. Many were supposed to have been caught while engaged in the act of signalling to German bombers in order to direct them on to their targets, an operation which, were it true, carried with it certain fairly obvious hazards! It was left to the reader to decide whether all spies were women or whether all women were spies.

The 3rd Battalion City of Dundee Home Guard based at Telephone House in Ward Road was drawn from Post Office staff and had the role of defending Post Offices and Telephone Exchanges. Associated with this battalion was a platoon made up of employees of D. C. Thomson's.

Despite the stirring photographs of veterans of the battle of Omdurman staring, rheumy-eyed, down the barrel of a rifle, the stories of men standing guard with broomsticks and spears have a basis in fact. At the height of the invasion scare all that stood between St Andrews and an invading Nazi horde were 1,440 men armed with 360 rifles and ten rounds per gun. An appeal for weapons brought forth such things as 'a fearsome looking Arab flintlock'! As one contemporary newsreel put it: 'Thank God Abyssinia is with us!'

By the following year, though, matters had improved somewhat both in terms of equipment and training; some Home Guardsmen who had shown a particular aptitude as marksmen, were being trained as 'parashots' to shoot down enemy paratroopers in the air. At Ladybank, amid great secrecy, the anonymously titled 'Auxiliary Units' were being trained. These were parties of hand-picked men with particular skills in, for example, field craft, who would operate as saboteurs behind enemy lines in the event of invasion.

Throughout the war the Government were to refuse to allow women to bear arms despite the bitter resentment this caused, particularly when it came to the Home Guard. In March 1942 Vera Norris of 4 Briarwood Terrace, Dundee, wrote to the Military Liaison Committee in support of a Women's Home Defence Unit saying that 'if young boys of seventeen are deemed competent to hold a rifle surely it is no time to refuse the help of women'.

In reality there was little that the Home Guard could have done to deter a determined invader. They had virtually no transport and could thus not be deployed to best advantage, they had no effective equipment with which to fight tanks and, as late as 1943, their communications still relied heavily on carrier pigeons. Given the record of the Wehrmacht in other countries they conquered, it is more likely that they would have been treated as terrorists and shot out of hand. There were also clear signs of exhaustion and undernourishment amongst men required to undertake both their civilian job and military duty on a civilian ration.

At first the LDVs were told that 'if they defend their post to the last man they will be making no mistake'. Later, a more realistic attitude is evident

Having taken up a position in Allan Street overlooking the Custom House Gate and the East Station, it is as well that these Norwegian sailors were not called upon to fire their rifles or, more particularly, the Lewis Gun as, holding them in this fashion they would be more likely to injure themselves than the enemy.

from the Standing Operating Instructions for the Angus Sub Area, 1941, which state that 'There will be no withdrawal but the Home Guard must be prepared to sidestep the enemy when confronted with overwhelming force and use guerilla tactics to harass the enemy particularly on his flanks which will be very vulnerable'.

Though never a truly credible defence against invasion, particularly at the time of great threat, the Home Guard was a valuable reserve of manpower which was able to release members of the regular forces from relatively mundane tasks such as coastwatching and guarding less sensitive installations. Once the threat of invasion had receded the 2nd Dundee Battalion were used to man the Castle Green Battery and two anti-aircraft batteries manned the guns around the city. Further, the sight of armed men on the streets provided a considerable boost to public morale when it was most needed. They were also a valuable resource during the many military training exercises which were mounted in the area.

Whilst, mercifully, and despite one very close call at the Harbour, there were no recorded tragic incidents such as those which took place elsewhere in which trigger-happy Home Guardsmen shot and killed wholly innocent civilians they thought were acting suspiciously, a number of comic episodes did occur. The Home Guard were empowered to examine the identity cards of all travellers including the police, and stopping the local bobby and treating him as a suspect became a national pastime. One Home Guard patrol resolved a dispute with a special constable by the simple expedient of arresting him.

'The possibility of enemy agents disguised as civilians must not be overlooked' (Operational Instructions for Exercise Rabbit). The official War Office caption for this photograph, taken in Lochee outside the DPM Dairy at the corner of Bank Street and High Street, reads: 'A Fifth Columnist disguised as a police constable is roughly handled by Home Guards in the suburbs of a town.'

On another occasion, during an exercise near St Andrews, a car containing the Heads of the various Civil Defence services was stopped and the bemused occupants ordered out at gunpoint 'wan by wan'. During the same exercise a staff officer from Scottish Command was held up at gunpoint 19 times. Each time, his language became progressively worse until when he reached his destination he was described as 'incoherent'! In March 1941 there was an invasion scare in Forfar when the cinema projectionist picked up the wrong slide and called out the Home Guard instead of informing the audience that the air raid alert was over.

In his address at the final parade of the Dundee Home Guard on Sunday, 3 December 1944, Lord Provost Garnet Wilson paid tribute to the 4,778 men then serving in the three battalions and two anti-aircraft batteries saying, 'I am not surprised to be informed of a cheerful indifference on the part of all ranks to any instructions not connected with blood and battle.'

The first major exercise to involve the Army, Navy and RAF along with the Home Guard and Civil Defence Services in the Dundee area was Exercise 'Rabbit' held on 9 and 10 August 1941. The Civil Defence services went into action at 1100 hours on 9 August in response to mock bombing raids by RAF aircraft which were designed to simulate a pre-invasion bombardment. Lunchtime on a Saturday was chosen because only then were the large number of volunteers who made up the various services available having finished work for the weekend.

The bombing was followed up by 'enemy' landings by men from the 52nd and 31st Divisions shortly after midnight and, within an hour, much of Broughty Ferry along with the eastern half of the city were in their hands. Large parts of the city were deemed by umpires to have been destroyed, including Caroline Port power station, much of the Harbour and City Square, and fires were said to be out of control in Bell and Symes, Briggs Oil Depot and on vessels in the river. The defenders were armed with nothing more dangerous than empty rifles and fireworks. Tin cans filled with stones were used to represent machine gun fire.

By Sunday morning communications had become swamped with over 900 messages on the Angus Sub Area Command telephone net alone, along with many more being delivered by Despatch Riders and pigeons. Far too much information was being transmitted, particularly by the Civil Defence services, most of which was many hours out of date and only partially complete. Untrained communicators, often unfamiliar with the use of the telephone, were sending messages which, in many cases, contradicted themselves and it

*As a Bren Gun Carrier emerges from Flights Lane on to Lochee High Street, Home Guardsmen con-
cealed behind J. H. Thomson's chemist shop demonstrate the questionable tactic of taking on any
sort of armoured vehicle with rifles.*

was noted that the first report of a 'bomb' falling in Dundee to reach Sub Area
Command in Forfar was almost six hours late. The District Commissioner's
Headquarters in Barrack Street was the source of many of the communications difficulties due to poor training and equipment. One message which
reached Sub Area Command stated that 506 cattle had been injured by
enemy aircraft when this should have read five or six.

The final indignity for District Commissioner Sir John Phin must have
been a raid by two 'saboteurs' disguised as telephone engineers on his Headquarters. Armed with false passes they got past the sentry at Friarfield House
and were guided by a messenger to the most sensitive part of the building.
Here they were left alone and, pulling a brick wrapped in brown paper from
their tool kit which the sentry had failed to search, they placed it under a
table in Phin's office. On it was a label stating that 'this is a time bomb due

Former and serving members of 4 Platoon, Lochee Home Guard, November 1944.
DUNDEE COURIER AND EVENING TELEGRAPH

to go off at 10.45 a.m.' They then left the building and were back at their base in Ward Road having completed the operation in well under 20 minutes.

Exercise 'Rabbit' finished just over an hour later at 1200 hours on Sunday, 10 August. It is not recorded whether the umpires decided that the defenders had been successful in repelling the invaders; possibly this would have been too damaging to morale!

Valuable lessons were learned during these exercises, which were held as often as once a month, and they provided experience for men who would find themselves involved in real street fighting in Europe during 1944/45. In Exercises 'Smoky I and II' attacks were mounted against Arbroath Airfield, and 'Peashooter II' involved attacks on Broughty Ferry Castle and the Stannergate. The plans for Exercise 'Tay' assumed, amongst other damage, an unexploded parachute mine lying on the deck of the Tay Ferry *B.L. Nairn*, a persistent gas bomb in the Queen's Hotel, over 100 dead in Taybridge

Station and 70 dead at Ancrum Road School along with 19,000 homeless. In Exercise 'Jam', which began in the early hours of Sunday, 30 May 1943, amid the roar of aircraft, explosions and clouds of smoke, a seaborne attack was mounted against Broughty Ferry Castle. The Home Guard managed to 'wipe out' the first wave of invaders though the castle was subsequently taken. In the fighting, one invader had captured three Home Guardsmen and was looking for somewhere to put his prisoners when one of them turned on him and, much to his embarrassment, disarmed him. During this exercise, wardens at Invergowrie were still using pigeons to report 'enemy' troop movements.

In the event, it was never necessary to issue the code word for invasion of the Angus coastline – selected by someone with heavy irony to be 'Gallipoli'.

Early morning, Sunday, 10 August 1941 and a Polish Matilda Tank at the bus stop at the top of Scoonieburn Hill on the Edinburgh Road, Perth. Hopelessly undergunned and poorly armoured, the Matilda tank stood little chance against superior German armour.

Others, such as 'Caterpillars', which denoted the landing of tanks, and 'Parasols', which signified landings by parachutists, were perhaps less imaginative. It is known that as part of his invasion plan, Operation Sealion, Hitler did plan to send two passenger liners as part of a convoy towards the north-east coast as a feint designed to draw off units of the Royal Navy. Ironically, one of these liners was to have been the *Europa* which had played a central role in the Jessie Jordan affair two years previously.

Chapter Five

Violent Fires in Dundee

At 1357 hours on Monday, 16 October 1939, green section, 602 (City of Glasgow) Squadron, Auxiliary Air Force, landed their Spitfires at Leuchars Airfield to refuel. They had spent the previous hour on patrol between May Island and Peterhead and, despite hearing enemy R/T chatter, had seen nothing. While the ground crew were working on their aircraft, Douglas Farquhar, Sandy Johnstone and Ian Ferguson sat down to a hasty lunch in the Officers Mess. At 1440 hours, the Station went on alert and everyone rushed to the shelters from where they watched three Blenheims making their way slowly towards Edinburgh.

'For Christ's sake get a move on – those aren't Blenheims – they're ruddy Germans!' With these memorable words Squadron Leader Farquhar led his men off to take part in the first aerial combat over the British Isles of the Second World War. During the subsequent action, George Pinkerton and Archie McKellar, also from 602 Squadron, shot down a Junkers 88 of Kampf Geschwader 30 between Crail and May Island after it had bombed the cruiser HMS *Southampton* at Rosyth. As Air Vice Marshal Sandy Johnstone recalls, Pinkerton later visited Helmut Pohle, the commander of this aircraft, in hospital. Undaunted by the fact that the German had lost his front teeth in the crash, he insisted on giving him a bag of toffees.

On 29 November 1939 Hitler's Führer Directive No. 9 named Dundee in a list of targets for both the Luftwaffe and the Kriegsmarine. Minor nuisance raids and minelaying began almost immediately. At the War Cabinet at 1130 hours on Tuesday, 5 December, Winston Churchill, then First Lord of the Admiralty, reported that the *Eskdene* (3829T) had been damaged by a mine east of the Bell Rock. At midday on 7 December, three Spitfires of blue section, 603 (City of Edinburgh) Squadron engaged seven Heinkel 111s south-east of Montrose, claiming two as 'damaged'. Two weeks later, 602 Squadron Spitfires from Drem brought down a Heinkel 111 after it was seen near the Bell Rock.

Fourth Officer Woods with crew members of the City of Marseilles *safely ashore in Dundee following the mine explosion which damaged their ship on 6 January 1940.*
DUNDEE COURIER AND EVENING TELEGRAPH

On the morning of Saturday, 6 January 1940, the Ellerman liner *City of Marseilles* (8300T), inbound from Calcutta with a cargo of jute, was damaged by a mine near the fairway buoy at the entrance to the Tay. Of the 163 crew, one Lascar seaman was killed and 14 were injured. On the bridge, Captain Olsen was thrown five feet in the air by the explosion which badly holed the ship on her starboard side. When the survivors abandoned ship, two of the lifeboats capsized, though fortunately the Pilot Cutter, the RAF launch from Tayport and two armed trawlers were on hand to pick up those struggling in the water. The ship was finally secured alongside the Eastern Wharf three days later, following which her cargo was removed and repairs completed.

On 9 January Spitfires were seen racing past Carnoustie in an attempt to intercept raiders which had sunk the D.P.&L. steamer *Gowrie* (689T) four miles east of Stonehaven. All 12 of the *Gowrie*'s crew were brought safely ashore. Three days later, red section of 602 Squadron and Hurricanes from 111 Squadron attacked and destroyed another Heinkel 111 off Carnoustie. One survivor, Leutnant G. Kahle, was brought ashore by the RAF Air-Sea Rescue Launch from Tayport.

At 0930 hours on 29 January a trawler was attacked in the estuary by a Heinkel 111 which was chased off by Hurricanes of red section, 609 Squadron. When this same aircraft was shot down over Wick some months later, the pilot recalled his earlier meeting with 609 Squadron, saying that he had only just made it back to base with a bullet-riddled aircraft.

During a snowstorm on Tuesday, 30 January, three vessels were attacked by one aircraft at the entrance to the river. Four bombs were dropped around the SS *Stancourt* after which the *City of Bath* and the Hull trawler *Lady Shirley* were repeatedly strafed. The *Stancourt* had to be run ashore on the Abertay Sands where she remained for almost a month while repairs were carried out. For days afterwards hams, butter and tinned food from her cargo were being washed up in St Andrews and Broughty Ferry.

The following day, during an attack which lasted almost 30 minutes, and with both his machine gunners wounded, Captain Prince of the *Otterpool* kept up return fire at the enemy aircraft with a rifle while laying on his back on the bridge deck. *Otterpool* was later sunk by a U-boat in the Bay of Biscay.

One week later an Estonian ship and regular visitor to the river with cargoes of paper, the SS *Anu*, was sunk by a mine. Thirteen survivors drifted ashore after 12 hours on a raft, though one of them, Elma Jorgensen, the ship's stewardess, later died, bringing the death toll to seven including Captain Raudsoo and his wife. Wreckage was spread over five miles of the Angus coastline.

On 9 February the hopper barge *Foremost 102* (833T) was off Arbroath when she was bombed and damaged by a Heinkel 111 which was chased into cloud by Green Section of 603 Squadron. Two of the *Foremost*'s crew were killed and the rest abandoned ship. They were picked up by the paddle steamer *Brighton Queen* which stood by as the ship was taken in tow by the Mine Sweeping Trawler *Equerry*. The *Foremost* had to be immediately dry docked when she was brought into Dundee four days later, whereupon one unexploded bomb and various incendiaries were removed from her. The *Brighton Queen*, a former excursion steamer converted for use as a minesweeper with the 7th Flotilla based at Rosyth, was sunk four months later during the Dunkirk evacuation.

The Spitfires of 603 (City of Edinburgh) Squadron operated from RAF Montrose from January to August 1940 when they left to take part in the Battle of Britain. Passing low over the dispersal point is Flight Lieutenant Boulter who would shoot down three Me 109s during the battle. Second Spitfire from the right, coded XT⊚M, is that of Flying Officer Richard Hillary, who was shot down in flames off Margate on 3 September 1940 and grievously burnt. While still convalescing in 1941 he wrote The Last Enemy, *his classic and vivid description of life in the RAF in those first months of the war. Having fought his way back to fitness, he returned to flying and was killed in a flying accident at Duns in Berwickshire on 8 January 1943.*
603 Squadron ended the war with a formidable tally of victories:
Aircraft: 250 confirmed; 121.3 probable; 167 damaged.
Shipping: 50 confirmed (7,845 tons); 6 probable (8,004 tons); 6 damaged (10,992 tons)
Squadron personnel were awarded 15 DFCs and five DFMs.
MONTROSE AERODROME MUSEUM SOCIETY

Red Section of 609 Squadron were in action again at 1300 hours on Tuesday, 27 February, shooting down a Heinkel 111 in flames off Fife Ness, after a chase from St Abbs Head. The four crew were picked up by the trawler *Shelomi* which was skippered by James Dickson of Broughty Ferry. Having consumed the supply of chocolate and cognac from their liferaft, one of the airmen told Skipper Dickson that 'Var ist no good' whereupon, seemingly determined to work his passage, he proceeded to help stoke the boiler. They were later handed over to the Admiralty drifter *Willow* and brought to Dundee where they were held in HMS *Unicorn* before being taken away by the military. After this action, which was 609 Squadron's first success of the war, Flying Officer Ayre counted 14 bullet holes in his aircraft. On 8 March, Ernst Breiler, the pilot of, and sole survivor from, a Heinkel 111 shot down the previous day, was brought ashore at Tayport by the RAF Air Sea Rescue launch.

The first major loss for Dundee occured early in March, when the trawler *Ben Attow* struck a mine seven miles west of May Island in the Forth and the crew of nine – men from Broughty Ferry, Monifieth and Tayport – were lost. One victim was the cook, Luigi Schiavetta. On only his second trip to sea, his son Joe was a member of the crew of the *Willow*. A distress fund was started for which the Rep Theatre gave benefit productions of George Bernard Shaw's *Candida* at Nicoll Street.

It had been decided that Dundee would be developed as a base for submarines and small craft but when the new Naval Officer in Charge, Captain Hurt, was appointed in January 1940 the situation was shambolic. Coastal defences were non-existent. Auxiliary patrols of small vessels were being established between Fife Ness and Johnshaven but, as Hurt put it in his report to the Admiralty, the vessels were wholly inadequate for their task. They were too old, too small and generally in poor condition. Constant repairs meant that it was proving impossible to keep up a regular patrol rota. This activity was conducted in the face of regular German attempts to block the river using mine-laying aircraft, often the Heinkel 115 floatplanes of Kuestenfliegergruppe 506 which would alight out at sea before taxi-ing inshore to drop their deadly cargoes. Following the German invasion of Norway in April 1940, most enemy aerial activity was undertaken by the Heinkel 111Hs of Kampfgeshwader 26 based at Stavanger, although the Junkers 88s of KG30 based at Aalborg in Denmark were also operating in the area. KG 26 was made up largely of naval personnel and its activities were primarily directed against shipping.

HMM/S *Gadfly*, formerly the trawler *Tenedos* (290T), exploded a mine in the Tay on Wednesday, 7 February 1940. On 27 July an aircraft was seen to drop two parachute mines into the Tay War Channel at Abertay and the following morning *Gadfly* was sent out in company with another converted trawler, HMM/S *Sturton*, to sweep them. Having searched all day and found nothing, they were hauling in the gear when one of the mines exploded between the ships, which were only 50 feet apart. Despite the crews having been blown flat on the deck there were no serious injuries and both vessels were towed in to Dundee. *Sturton* was only lightly damaged but *Gadfly* had begun to sink and had to be beached at the entrance to the Earl Grey Dock. She was immediately evacuated as her boiler was in danger of exploding. When dry docked for repair the following evening she was found to have damaged 30 plates in her hull and had her propellor blown off.

Early in the afternoon of 3 July, Green Section of 603 Squadron under Flying Officer Carbury intercepted a Junkers 88 over Montrose and shot it down into the sea. Three survivors were later picked up. Meanwhile, the auxiliary patrols were continuing, despite the attentions of the Luftwaffe and the worst the weather could throw at the launches and yachts used. At 0022 hours on Tuesday, 9 July, the yacht *Patricia* was on patrol off Arbroath when four bombs were dropped around her. Fortunately she was only slightly damaged and was able to make port under her own power with no casualties. The following day, Flight Lieutenant Urie of 602 Squadron shot down one JU 88 off Fife Ness, and Flying Officer Jack damaged another.

At 2230 hours on 15 September the Aberdeen fishing boat *Beathwood* and the Manchester Lines vessel *Nailsea River* (5548T), bound from Buenos Aires to the Tyne with wheat, were sunk one mile and four miles east of Montrose respectively. Eight miles north-east of Dunbar, aircraft from the same raid also bombed and sank the *Halland*, an ex-Danish coaster bound for Dundee with a cargo of cement from London.

At lunchtime on 23 December 1940 a Heinkel 111 dropped a bomb in the sea 300 yards off St Andrews harbour. Immediately afterwards it was engaged with 12-pounder and machine gun fire by two minesweeping trawlers, *Southern Foam* and *Southern Field*, and chased off.

At 1100 hours on 7 February 1941 the *Bay Fisher* (575T) was bombed and sunk less than four miles north-east of the Bell Rock. Four survivors were picked up by HMS *Heliopolis* and brought to Dundee. On 7 March a KG 26 Heinkel 111 (1H + HH) was attacking the trawler *Strathblane* off Buddon Ness when it hit the ship's mast and crashed into the sea. This aircraft had been plotted over Arbroath at 1953 hours, after which it flew south-west and circled over Buddon Ness Lighthouse before attacking at 2002 hours. One of its crew was found dead and the remaining three listed as missing. On the

Strathblane there were no casualties though two unexploded bombs were found lying on deck which were later dumped at sea. Exactly a year before this incident, the *Strathblane* had been witness to the explosion which claimed the *Ben Attow*.

At 1935 hours on 11 March 1941, convoy EN 84 was passing the mouth of the Tay when it was attacked by at least two Heinkel 111s. The first attack was made on the lead ship of the port column, SS *Jamaica Producer*, and again the Heinkel struck its victim's mast, leaving four feet of its starboard tailplane lying on the ship's deck. Lieutenant Commander Robert Aubrey, commander of the escort in HMS *Fowey*, reported that this aircraft made off towards St Andrews losing height rapidly. Off Tentsmuir it came under fire from a Beaufort of 42 Squadron, Coastal Command and crashed into the sea. Two further attacks were made despite heavy anti-aircraft fire at 1954 hours and 2000 hours during which three bombs were dropped close to the SS *Royal Star* without causing any damage or casualties. At 2200 hours that night Coastguards reported flares in St Andrews Bay and, an hour later, three survivors from the crashed Heinkel were picked up by HMM/S *Gadfly*. Six days later, an aircraft torpedoed and sank a Norwegian freighter, the SS *Einar Jarl* near the Bell Rock. One Greek crewman was lost after he went back to his cabin to collect personal effects.

The heaviest raid against a convoy in the area was mounted by approximately six Heinkel 111 aircraft of KG 26 on 3 April 1941. It left two ships sunk and a further two damaged. The *Geddington Court* (6,903T) was damaged by bombing and strafing seven miles east of the Bell Rock, as was the *Assuan* (499T) immediately off the entrance to Montrose. The *Cairnie* (250T) was sunk by bombs five miles east of Johnshaven, and the *Croomaum* (748T) disappeared with all hands off Montrose at around the same time. The circumstances of her loss are unknown although it is probable that she met the same fate. Three weeks later, on 24 April, the motor vessel *Dolius* (5,507T) was bombed and strafed 12 miles east of Auchmithie and, the following evening, the Norwegian minesweeping trawler *Doerland* was strafed at Barry Buddon.

Around this time, in the Spring of 1941, the number of friendly aircraft being fired on by armed merchant ships in the area was causing the RAF understandable concern. A number of occasions when naval gunners had been too 'quick on the draw' led Fighter Command to point out forcibly that fighters could not fire recognition signals and that, in any event, all single-engined aircraft were obviously friendly.

The morning of Wednesday, 12 March 1941 and two of the crew of the Heinkel which came down the previous evening at Tentsmuir are marched along Bell Street to the Drill Hall.
DUNDEE COURIER AND EVENING TELEGRAPH

At around midnight on 5 June the auxiliary patrol vessel *River Lossie* was bombed and machine gunned at the entrance to the Tay, returning fire with her Lewis gun. A few minutes later the SS *Queensbury* and the S S *Taurus* were attacked near Montrose. *Queensbury* was ablaze from stem to stern when her crew were rescued by the Montrose Lifeboat and, after capsizing, was sunk by gunfire. *Taurus* also sank after her crew were picked up by a drifter.

The Admiralty tug *Buccaneer* was off the entrance to Montrose, towing a battle practice target from the range at Lunan Bay, in a strong gale on 9 November 1941. At 1815 hours, while waiting for the sea to moderate so that she could enter harbour, she was bombed. Three sticks of bombs came down alongside her with one direct hit passing through her deck and out through her side, fortunately without exploding. Damage from this and the effect of near misses caused the vessel to start making water, and fires were started on deck by tracer bullets. With her engine having broken down, the *Buccaneer* eventually ran aground near the entrance to the North Esk river where her crew of 43 were rescued by breeches buoy. Meanwhile, Montrose Lifeboat had been launched but, owing to the steadily worsening conditions, was unable to help. Having spent the night at sea, she capsized while attempting to re-enter Montrose at 1300 hours the following day, and three crewmen, including the Coxswain, were washed overboard. Fortunately, they were still alive when dragged ashore.

In the early evening of 8 December 1941, Heinkel 111s attacked a group of four minesweeper trawlers as they entered Lunan Bay to anchor for the night. Two, the *Milford Earl* and the *Phineas Beard,* were sunk with the loss of 17 officers and men killed and a further five wounded.

One of the worst incidents of the war in the Tay estuary took place on Thursday, 12 March 1942. The former Southern Railway pleasure steamer HMS *St Briac*, a 2,300-ton Fleet Air Arm Target and Navigation Training Vessel attached to the air station at Arbroath, had sailed from the Eastern Wharf, Dundee, that morning. By mid-afternoon she was sending out distress signals while drifting into the offshore minefield in appalling weather. The crew abandoned ship and one lifeboat was picked up by the tug *Empire Larch*. The other lifeboat drifted north, finally capsizing and driving ashore at 0950 hours the next day near Collieston, where 13 out of the 17 occupants drowned. In all, 47 officers and men were lost that night.

The first bombs to fall on land in the area came down at Friarton in Perth on 26 June 1940 when one aircarft dropped four high explosive bombs and a number of incendiaries at the Moncrieff Railway Tunnel. At 0039 hours on 28 June two 250kg bombs fell on fields at Leyshade Farm at Tealing and, 20 minutes later, another aircraft passed over the north of the city prior to dropping another four bombs 250 yards south of a searchlight detachment at Balbinny Farm, Muirdrum. That night more than 14 enemy aircraft were operating between the Forth and Montrose, and as far inland as Crieff.

On 13 July four bombs fell near Rossie Priory, Inchture, with high explosive bombs and incendiaries also falling at Ladybank and Newburgh. Four bombs were jettisoned at sea off Arbroath, and the following day a German communiqué claimed damage to Dundee docks.

The first fatalities occurred on the morning of 18 July 1940 when Montrose airfield was bombed. Two RAF personnel were killed and nine wounded, 13 aircraft were damaged, two of which were written off. In addition to service personnel, a Mrs Wilson of Broomfield was killed by blast while feeding her chickens. The enemy aircraft involved had been plotted from Inverurie and was chased off by a Spitfire from 603 Squadron. A further attack on Montrose airfield took place on 23 July when one 500kg bomb was dropped without causing any casualties. The HE 111 responsible had previously passed over Barry and Arbroath where it had dropped bombs in the sea. One week later green section of 603 Squadron claimed a Heinkel shot down into the sea off Montrose.

Friday, 2 August saw the first bombs fall in the city itself during a night of considerable enemy activity over central Scotland. Just afer midnight, one aircraft dropped 23 50kg bombs around Linlathen House. It had previously dropped four bombs at Murroes near Kellas and another eight at East Pit-kerro Farm on Drumsturdy Road which shook a nearby searchlight post and disabled its generator. The only casualty was a prowling cat at Linlathen House, where the housekeeper, Miss Hughes, reported that the whole house shook, plaster fell from ceilings and windows were blown in. Bombs were also dropped that night on Glens Poultry Farm near Strathkinnes in Fife. Just over 24 hours later, four bombs fell on 8 and 15 holdings at Tealing. During the following Sunday night a further ten exploded in the Tannadice area, at Craigieassie and Miltonbank.

For the next ten days the enemy concentrated their efforts on minelaying in the estuary until, at 0355 hours on Thursday, 15 August a Heinkel 115 floatplane S4 + BH was picked up by the beams of searchlights from Barry Buddon and Ardownie. It came in from the sea at around 1,000 feet and machine gunned the post at Ardownie as it passed. Turning, it dived down the beam of the searchlight to around 300 feet, firing its forward facing machine gun, before levelling out and dropping a 250kg bomb which exploded a short distance away. As Major Norman Woodburn, the commanding officer of 417 Searchlight Battery, wrote, 'The site was pretty well peppered with machine gun bullets.' Nobody was injured, however, though some equipment was damaged. The raider was then picked up by another searchlight post at Kirkton of Monikie which it strafed from a height of around 60 feet. Here again nobody was injured though one bullet landed at the feet of the Detachment Commander.

Meanwhile, Bombardier Reid, Detachment Commander of the post at Balbinnie, had ordered his Lewis gunner, Lance Bombardier Trench, to man his gun, and had deployed his searchlight in the direction of the enemy aircraft. When he switched on, the Heinkel was only 150 yards from him, very

Interior of a flat occupied by cattleman Charles Brown and his family at Linlathen House after the attack on Friday, 2 August 1940. Fortunately, the room was unoccupied at the time of the bombing.

low, and caught full in the beam. Lance Bombardier Trench and the gunner in the aircraft exchanged fire before it disappeared from view. Shortly afterwards the sound of the aircraft's engines were heard to stop and, when daylight came, wreckage was found a mile away in a field at Faldiehill Farm, Arbirlot. Despite the claim of the Lewis gunner to have shot it down, it became clear that the pilot had in fact been blinded by the searchlight. Two of the crew, namely the pilot, Oberfw. Holfert and the gunner, Fw. Schroers, were killed in the crash and were buried with full military honours at Arbroath East Cemetery. The aircraft commander and navigator, Lieutenant sur zee Tonne, although seriously injured, survived and was taken to Arbroath Infirmary.

Following a raid on Montrose on the night of 25/26 August in which four people were killed, at 0017 hours on 28 August eight bombs were dropped at

On Tuesday, 13 August 1940, under the title 'Adler Tag', the Luftwaffe launched attacks against Fighter Command airfields in southern England, the phase of the Battle of Britain which brought them closest to success. Two days later, on Thursday, 15 August a series of diversionary attacks were mounted against east-coast targets in the mistaken belief that they would cause the RAF to draw off some of its depleted resources to protect these areas.

That afternoon both KG 26 and KG 30 took part in costly raids against targets in Yorkshire in which they each lost eight aircraft along with seven escorting ME 110 fighter bombers of ZG 76. Earlier, the first of these feints had been flown by the Heinkel 115 floatplanes of Keustenfleigergruppe 506, each aircraft carrying one bomb which the crews called their visiting card.

At 0355hrs one Heinkel began a series of attacks on searchlight detachments between Monifeith and Arbroath, during which it crashed into high ground at Faldiehill Farm, Arbirlot. Wreckage, including the starboard tailplane seen here, was spread over two fields. The sole survivor from the crew, the aircraft's commander and navigator, told his interrogators that he had been convinced that he was over the Montrose area, 15 miles further north.

AFTER THE BATTLE PUBLICATIONS

Monifieth. One fell on Milton Mill, which was being used as billets for the Black Watch, leaving one soldier dead and four wounded.

One bomb was dropped near Muirdrum at 0050 hours on 4 September 1940, and three days later, at 2000 hours on Saturday, 7 September, the invasion imminent codeword 'Cromwell' was issued. Some units were completely unaware of what 'Cromwell' meant and others, including the searchlight detachments around Dundee, issued live ammunition and stood to all night without realising that the message had been sent to them for information only. Action on it was only required of forces in south-east England.

At around 0200 hours on Wednesday, 25 September, a number of enemy aircraft were passing over the city and north-east Fife on their way home from raids on central Scotland. At 0233 hours one aircraft dropped two 250kg bombs, one of which exploded on the junction of Dalkeith Road and Nesbitt Street, the other landing on what was then a vegetable patch at Montgomerie Crescent. At Dalkeith Road a large crater was made in the street and some damage done to houses by blast and flying debris but nobody was injured. One bomb also exploded that night at Craigfoodie, 150 yards west of Moonzie Burn Bridge on the Dairsie to Balmullo road in Fife, and flares were dropped over Leuchars Airfield.

October began with a raid at Montrose when four bombs were dropped around Sunnyside Asylum. Four patients and two nurses were injured. Six years later one of the nurses on duty was awarded the George Medal for bravery during this raid. Over the next ten days bombs fell at Mains of Kellie

Corporation officials and a policeman survey the crater in Baxter Park on Tuesday, 5 November 1940. Taybank Works is top left.
DUNDEE COURIER AND EVENING TELEGRAPH

at Arbirlot, West Scryne Farm at Panbride, number 15 holding Tealing and Goudie by Arbirlot. On 8 and 11 October enemy aircraft were plotted over Arbroath and Leuchars engaged in minelaying and, on the latter occasion when four bombs were dropped at Inverkeillor, one fighter was scrambled but no contact made.

In the early evening of Friday 25 October, around eight aircraft from KG 26 commenced a series of attacks on targets in the area. At 1830 hours three He 111s flew low across Montrose dropping eighteen bombs along with a large number of incendiaries, and strafing the town.

Damage was mainly confined to the harbour and the area around the airfield, although a number of buildings were also damaged by machine gun fire. At Wharf Street jetty the Admiralty drifter *Duthies* and the fishing vessel *Janet* were sunk, three of the crew of the former being injured. One bomb also hit the nearby Chivers jam factory causing extensive damage.

At the airfield two bombs exploded alongside the railway at the main entrance to the station and severely damaged a row of cottages. A further three bombs all but demolished two hangars, the Officer's Mess and a number of other buildings. Six RAF personnel were killed and twenty injured. Eight aircraft were destroyed and another ten damaged. Four bombs exploded on the links causing no damage and five unexploded bombs were found, three on the airfield and two at Rossie Island. Having strafed St Cyrus, the Heinkels circled back over Montrose where they again machine gunned the town and a southbound express train.

Four Hurricanes from 111 Squadron managed to get airborne, one of which opened fire on the enemy but, in the gathering gloom, no hits were recorded.

Ten minutes later two Heinkels came in from the sea at around 100 feet and attacked the Naval air station at Arbroath. As it was nearly dark they were able to switch on their navigation lights and join the training aircraft in the circuit without being noticed. They caught the airfield defences completely by surprise when they swooped down and dropped twelve bombs, six of which failed to explode, and a large number of incendiaries. Though there was some damage to buildings, there were no casualties.

As these aircraft departed out to sea the defences came to life. One was caught in the beam of two searchlights and was attacked with Lewis Gun fire after which it was seen to be swaying and losing height. It was claimed as a ''probable''. By this time the fires at RAF Montrose could be seen twelve miles away in Friockheim. The following morning a parachute mine was found hanging from a tree beside the main road past the airfield.

Some minutes later eight bombs were dropped at Cellardyke near Anstruther. Two people, a twelve year old boy and his mother, were killed and a number injured.

The final attack of the evening began at around 1905 hours when a stick of four bombs were dropped on open ground between Boarhills and Brownhills. This aircraft also dropped four bombs in St Andrews. They fell in the Kinness Burn, Alison Place, Westburn Lane and in St Mary's Quad. The bomb in the Kinness Burn caused little damage but that in Alison Place bounced off the street and exploded in the back garden of Greenside Dairy Cottage, which was demolished. Fortunately the elderly woman who lived there was out at the time. The explosion in Westburn Lane caused considerable damage to the Bute Medical building and that in St Mary's Quad blew out the windows of the Carnegie Library. The suction effect which followed the initial blast sucked a number of books out into the crater.

A Repair Party at work restoring Dalkeith Road. The house at the top right has its windows covered with anti-shatter tape against injury from flying glass and, notably, they are unbroken.
DUNDEE COURIER AND EVENING TELEGRAPH

It was particularly fortunate that there were no casualties in St Andrews as, owing to a power failure, it had not been possible to sound the siren when the "red warning" was received at 1850 hours.

Four bombs were dropped at Arbroath on 16 October, and Saturday, 26 October 1940 saw a number of flares being dropped over Dundee and Invergowrie during a busy night when there were three separate air raid warnings. Altogether, there were seven air raid warnings in 76 hours that weekend, totalling five hours and 48 minutes. The following Friday bombs fell at Kinglassie, and on farm land north of Leuchars. At Craigie Farm a crater 86 yards in circumference and 12 feet deep was made 500 yards west of the farm buildings.

On Monday, 4 November 1940, over 30 German aircraft crossed the city, and at 2104 hours one plane dropped two bombs which exploded harmlessly in fields beside Drumgeith Cottages. It then dropped a 1000kg bomb near the south-east corner of Baxter Park and a final 1000kg in soft ground at the rear of Taybank Works on Arbroath Road. The bomb in Baxter Park fell on part of a trench shelter, which was fortunately unoccupied, creating a 15-foot deep crater. Shelter Warden John Campbell was standing close by but was uninjured. Trees were uprooted and rocks thrown a considerable distance, one boulder falling through the ceiling of a top flat belonging to James Morrison on the opposite side of Arbroath Road. Windows were broken over a wide area including those in Glebelands School, Baffin Street, Eden Street and Baxter Park Terrace.

The bomb at the rear of Taybank Works first demolished part of a high wall, glanced off the side of an underground shelter which contained around 60 women mill workers before coming to rest, fortunately without exploding, 20 feet underground. Almost immediately, an agitated voice came on the line to Dundee Telephone Exchange asking for the Fire Brigade and Ambulance. Calmly, the operator asked whether there was a fire or if there were casualties and the voice replied 'There's nae fire and naebody hurt but for God's sake send something – we've been bombed!'

On examining the scene that night, a Bomb Reconnaissance Officer confirmed the general belief that a small bomb had indeed exploded. What followed may have had some bearing on the fact that this same officer threw himself in front of a London tube train some days later.

Knowledge of the likely bomb load of the aircraft and a study of the scene led Peter Fletcher to suspect otherwise. On entering the shelter he noticed that the light filaments were still intact and realised that the bomb had not

Surprisingly little damage was done to houses by the bomb at the corner of Nesbitt Street and Dalkeith Road on 25 September 1940, although large lumps of tarmac fell through the roof of the Inglis family's house (left), with one piece a yard square coming to rest in the hall. Some ceilings were cracked and a number of windows broken, but the blast was largely absorbed by soft clay.
DUNDEE COURIER AND EVENING TELEGRAPH

exploded. Picking up a piece of metal lying nearby, he took it to the metallurgist at the University College, the appropriately named Dr Steel, who confirmed that it was part of a German bomb. In the event the bomb's presence was not reported to 93 Bomb Disposal Unit Royal Engineers until 27 November. Operations to remove it were hampered by the presence of an underground spring, and only late on the following day was the fuse uncovered, revealing markings which identified it as a 1000kg anti-shipping bomb nicknamed in honour of the Reichsmarschall Goering's corpulent figure, 'Hermann'.

Over three weeks after it was dropped, the unexploded bomb is removed from Taybank Works.
FROM THE COLLECTION OF PETER FLETCHER

SC 1000 U SD 1400

Further markings on the casing confirmed its identity:

Nur – Schlo B1000
Sk Lief 31/37
10690

The bomb was eventually extracted with the help of a Corporation crane on the 30 November and taken to Lumley Den by lorry. Unsuccessful attempts were made to remove the fuse and it was exploded later that day with what was described by one observer as a 'hell of a bang'. The owners of Taybank Works gave the Bomb Disposal Unit a cricket set as a mark of their gratitude.

The morning after this raid, as the *Courier* accused the Corporation of 'fiddling while Rome burns', Secretary of the Chamber of Commerce, George Donald, was registering a 'strong protest' with the Secretary of State for Air, Sir Archibald Sinclair, saying that 'only last night an aircraft circled the city for three hours before dropping four bombs, and not a gun was fired'. The truth was that, other than a few searchlights, there were no anti-aircraft defences around Dundee at the time. The two batteries of AA guns that had been mounted around the city at the outbreak of the war had been removed to provide cover for the more vulnerable areas in the south, and no barrage balloons had been provided. Whilst AA guns were never particularly effective, the sound of them firing at enemy aircraft did bring about a marked improvement in the morale of the population of bombed areas.

That even a small number of bombs, allied to lack of sleep caused by frequent alerts and overwork, was having a significant effect on morale in the city can be seen from Donald's letter when he says that, without protection, workers had indicated that they would not carry on working after the pre-liminary alert and until the aircraft in the vicinity warning stopped as the Government had requested. Sinclair's Private Secretary replied to the effect

No. 13 Briarwood Terrace, the morning after, looking into the wreckage of No. 11, which belonged to solicitor Patrick Duncan and was subsequently demolished. The Duncans were fortunately visiting friends further along the terrace at the time of the attack.
FROM THE COLLECTION OF PETER FLETCHER

that there were no guns available and bluntly pointed out that there were more important places to the war effort than Dundee!

At 2000 hours that night, Tuesday, 5 November 1940, wireless sets in Dundee were being tuned in to the start of Cyril Fletcher's popular programme *Thanking Yew*; at the Forest Park Cinema the audience were settling in to watch Anne Rutherford and Frank Morgan in *The Ghost Comes Home*; and, at the ARP Training School in Dudhope Park, a group of undertakers were being instructed in the handling of bodies contaminated by poison gas. The first house of the evening at the Odeon in Strathmartine Road were making their way through the blackout on a showery night after watching Will Fyffe and Phyllis Calvert in the prophetically titled *They Came By Night*.

At 2006 hours the distinctive sound of an enemy aircraft off to the southwest was punctuated both by the sirens and, at almost the same instant, the first of a series of eight explosions in the west end of the city. The bombs, all of which were 250kg high explosive, had fallen in two sticks of four. They came down on open ground on the west side of Farington Terrace, in the

Briarwood Terrace, viewed from the rear.
FROM THE COLLECTION OF PETER FLETCHER

garden at the back of Fernbrae Nursing Home, at 13 Briarwood Terrace, in front of 12 Marchfield Road, at the back of 258 Blackness Road, into 19 Rosefield Street, on the pavement outside the electricity sub-station in Forest Park Place and into part of Queen Victoria Works in Brook Street.

The first bomb to cause serious damage or casualties was that on 13 Briarwood Terrace. Here the bomb exploded in the front of the house which collapsed, bringing with it much of the houses on either side. Joists were thrown into the air to fall through the roofs of other houses 200 feet along the terrace. The occupier, the Rev. Andrew Moodie, minister of Tay Square Church, and his daughter had taken shelter in the cellar along with their housekeeper, Mrs Elizabeth Cooper, Mrs Moodie being out on canteen duty at the time. When the rescue parties arrived some minutes later they found Andrew Moodie with a leg injury and his daughter who was uninjured. Miss Moodie stayed to help in the search for Mrs Cooper, who was found dead after a two-hour search. Fortunately, the houses on either side, though seriously damaged, were unoccupied and were later demolished.

The next bomb had landed in the garden ten feet from the front door of 12 Marchfield Road, the home of Mr and Mrs Alex Nicholl who were in the house with their daughter Eva and Mrs Nicholl's sister, a Miss Gonella. On hearing the first explosions, all four were running out of the house to the shelter in the back garden when the bomb struck. They were uninjured. The house was moved approximately two feet back off its foundations by the blast. Miss Gonella, a warden, reported to her post a short while later.

At Blackness Road the bomb exploded beside the wash houses in the rear of the tenement, 30 feet from an air raid shelter which was undamaged apart from minor cracking. It was fortunate that the siren had not sounded minutes earlier, as people would have been caught in the open heading for the shelter at the time.

The bomb in Rosefield Street crashed into the front room of the flat on the south side of the close at number 19 before exploding. The blast blew the walls out with the result that the roof and floors collapsed on top of each other. John Forbes, who lived on the top floor, told a *Courier* reporter that he heard a loud bang and then found himself standing almost on fresh air. Two large pieces of rubble were blown over the tenement on the other side of the street and on to the Logie School where they damaged the Art and Science rooms.

First ARP personnel on the scene were wardens Joe Good and Bert Cross from the post in Logie School. Four minutes after the explosion Joe Good

Bomb crater in the garden of Fernbrae Nursing Home, November 1940.
FROM THE COLLECTION OF PETER FLETCHER

was back at the wardens post with a situation report. At 2012 hours another warden came in with a situation report from the explosion in Blackness Road, only to find that the telephones had been cut. Fortunately, the police were on hand to transmit the warden's messages to the Western Division Report and Control Centre. Meanwhile, Auxiliary Fire Service personnel had arrived at Rosefield Street along with First Aid and Rescue parties.

In all, 11 people were released alive from the building, including 17-year-old Alex Grieg, who was trapped by beams across his head and body, a Polish soldier, who had been visiting his girlfriend, six-year-old Jean Forbes, a London evacuee, and 68-year-old John Laing, who had sustained a broken leg and arm and who was saved by the joists having fallen at an oblique angle. Mr Laing's wife Mary was found dead in the wreckage of their first floor flat by Auxiliary Fireman W. Marr. Strapped to a ladder, she was passed down to the waiting ambulance crew who took her body to the makeshift mortuary at Ryehill Church Hall in Mid Wynd.

Though the injured were dealt with efficiently by the Hawkhill First Aid Post and the Blinshall Street mobile unit, there were some confusion as dazed and shocked people received contradictory instructions. Most were told first to go to the Rest Centre at Logie School where there were hot refreshments and emergency accommodation, only for that to be countermanded later by someone else telling them to go to relatives or friends nearby. In fact, as the *People's Journal* reported later that week, not one of the 26 families made homeless turned up at the Rest Centre. This did create difficulties in ascertaining whether anyone was still missing, and not until his son came looking for him was it realised that Robert Coventry (66) had not been found. In the event his body was not recovered until 1100 hours on 7 November, 39 hours after the explosion.

In his report of the incident a Ministry of Home Security Intelligence Officer was unstinting in his praise for the various emergency services, making particular mention of the Rescue Parties who worked through the night in relays 'under dangerous and arduous conditions and did everything humanly possible to recover the remaining trapped victim'. He also said that people bore their misfortune with commendable courage, neighbours and others doing everything to assist those made homeless. Altogether that night

No. 12 Marchfield Road.
DUNDEE COURIER AND EVENING TELEGRAPH

109

41 First Aid Parties, 26 ambulances, 30 First Aid Party and casualty cars, 21 Rescue Squads and 6 Decontamination Squads turned out in addition to the Police and Fire Service.

The bomb in Forest Park Place fell on the pavement slightly to the east of the electricity sub station, only yards from the Forest Park Cinema which had a full house of 250 people at the time. In the cinema there was no panic although a few people fainted. The highly inflammable nitrate film flew off the projector spools but the projectionist had the presence of mind to take the necessary precautions. Gas, water and electricity supplies were disrupted over a large area of the west end, but at the Rep Theatre, after some community singing, the performance of *The Dominant Sex* carried on in candlelight.

The last bomb of the raid to fall within the city came down in an almost unoccupied area of Queen Victoria Works, lightly injuring two men. Another aircraft from the same formation dropped a stick of four bombs on open ground at Philpie Farm and Grange at Monifieth, two of which failed to explode. Later that night four bombs fell at Ruthven, and three near Glamis, one at Knockenny and two half a mile south-east of Arniefoul Farm. The two at Arniefoul Farm were 500kg bombs, both of which failed to explode. They were found in an old quarry the following morning by farm worker John Shepherd and he reported their presence to the police, who passed the information on to 93 Bomb Disposal Unit.

The all clear sounded at 2142 hours. A German communiqué issued the next day claimed that the Luftwaffe had started 'violent fires in Dundee'. Twelve days later a lecture was given for ARP personnel in the Kinnaird Picture House entitled 'The Psychology of Fear and Panic'.

Two weeks later, on 19 November, an aircraft which had been plotted by the radar at Douglas Wood while going south from Arbroath to the Forth and returning over Methil and Kinross, dropped one bomb which exploded 25 yards north of Cliff Cottage at Chesterhill House by Tayport, wrecking it. Two fighters were scrambled but failed to make contact and the aircraft disappeared off the plot, going out to sea from Carnoustie at around 1945 hours.

Apart from the regular reconnaissance flights, December and January 1941 were relatively quiet months.

At 1028 hours on 12 February a Junkers 88 crashed into Cunmont Hill in Pitairlie Wood near Newbigging. It was on an anti-shipping raid and had strafed the Port War Signal Station at Buddon Ness before being brought down by naval gunfire. The crew of four were killed. Later that day, 93 Bomb Disposal Unit were called out to deal with two bombs lying near the

No. 258 Blackness Road.
FROM THE COLLECTION OF PETER FLETCHER

Children playing in the crater at the back of No. 258 Blackness Road.
FROM THE COLLECTION OF PETER FLETCHER

wreck. One, a 500kg, was defused and emptied, the other, a 250kg, was blown up where it lay. That weekend, a train on the east coast main line was strafed, as were four lorries near Forfar.

On 19 February there were two red alerts, at 1024 hours and 1824 hours, and enemy aircraft were heard over Arbroath at 0955 hours, 1700 hours and 1907 hours.

That month, two soldiers were killed by mines which had drifted ashore, as were a further six at Montrose. In addition, children were being killed and injured by explosions, particularly of 'butterfly' anti-personnel bombs which went off when tampered with.

At 2050 hours on 9 March five 250kg bombs fell at Scotscraig, one in a field beside Scotscraig House and four on open ground at Nether Wood, Kirkton Barns. It was noted that a bus to St Andrews was passing at the time with all its lights on.

On 13 March more than 100 enemy aircraft were passing directly over the Stirling Park housing scheme in Dundee from 2243 hours until 0055 hours the next morning, and considerable anti-aircraft fire could be heard from the Forth. This was the start of the Clydebank blitz. The sirens sounded at 2201 hours with the first all clear coming at 0136 hours on 14 March, followed by a further red alert as the first wave of returning aircraft crossed the city. The all clear sounded again at 0621 hours, only to be followed by a further alert that evening at 2125 hours as further raids were mounted against what would become the most heavily bombed town in Britain during the war.

On 14 March, 44 Dundee Firemen were sent to Clydebank to assist, and the St Andrews Firemaster was warned that his pump should be ready to go there for emergency duty. That night a red light signalling C.A. repeatedly from Leuchars caused a scare. It later turned out that this was a landing signal for the Hudsons of 107 Squadron returning from Operation 'Bottle', raids against German shipping targets in Haugesund, Norway. As the Luftwaffe continued its assault on the Clyde Valley on the 15th and 16th, the only bombs to fall in the Dundee area were six jettisoned by a returning aircraft on farm land at Huntingfaulds by Tealing on the 16th at 2038 hours. On 22 March five bombs were jettisoned into the river between 2150 hours and 2202 hours and, the following day, 111 Squadron claimed a JU 88 as 'damaged' over Montrose. At breakfast time on 1 April, a lone raider machine gunned the Bell Rock.

The first alert on 7 April 1941 was at 1501 hours and, seven minutes later, one 250kg bomb was dropped near Baldovan House, Emmock Road, followed

Rosefield Street, the aftermath.
DUNDEE COURIER AND EVENING TELEGRAPH

Rosefield Street and Rescue Parties searching in the wreckage for Robert Coventry.
FROM THE COLLECTION OF PETER FLETCHER

by four more at Carlungie by Monikie, two of which failed to explode. 93 BDU later identified these as having delayed action fuses and they were allowed to destroy themselves. The all clear sounded at 1515 hours. That night the sirens sounded at 2154 hours for what would be the longest alert of the war, when over 140 enemy aircraft passed over the east coast, the all clear not being signalled until 0457 hours the following day. During the night, 20 incendiaries were jettisoned on farm land at Middlebank, Inchture, followed by a further 150 also on open ground at nearby Weston Farm. Heavy raids on central Scotland also led to a number of high explosive and incendiary bombs landing in Fife.

Eight bombs were dropped in the river off Balmerino pier at 0210 hours on 6 May, and at 1605 hours the next afternoon two Hurricanes from 'A' flight of 43 Squadron based at Drem intercepted a Junkers 88 4U + KH which was engaged on weather reconnaissance over Dundee. In the running chase which ensued, houses at 27 Seymour Street, 51 Blackness Avenue and 8 Cherryfield Lane were damaged by stray gunfire. Pilot Officer Cotton in Z2577 and Sergeant Lister in Z2638 saw pieces coming off the enemy aircraft over the river and claimed it as 'damaged'. Their claim was subsequently confirmed as 'destroyed' when the Royal Observer Corps saw the same aircraft crash into the sea off St Abbs Head.

The following evening, 13 Group plotters estimated that more than 225 enemy aircraft were operating in their area. On the morning of 10 May at 0249 hours seven bombs exploded at Mains of Fullarton, Meigle, as over 30 enemy aircraft operated between Whitby and the Tay and, at 0020 hours on 16 May 1941, three bombs exploded harmlessly on the shore near a coastal artillery position at Montrose.

On 27 May 1941 a Mrs Clark of India Lane, Montrose, was killed when her bungalow was demolished by a bomb dropped by a low flying Heinkel 111. One unexploded bomb was found nearby in India Street. It had struck the gable of a house and ricocheted past a woman hanging up her washing before coming to rest in a wash house. Local residents were immediately cleared from the area which was then guarded by Polish soldiers. After being seen using it as a card table, these men decided to remove the bomb so that people could return to their homes. Placing it in a barrow, they took it across the nearby railway line by the pedestrian bridge and out on to the Links. Only then were they told that it would have to be returned to its original position in the wash house! It was finally disposed of two days later by 93 Bomb Disposal Unit.

On 27 June Dowrie Works at Arbirlot was the target for two bombs which caused considerable damage, and one bomb was dropped in the sea off Leuchars Airfield at 0015 on 10 July by a lone Heinkel 111. This aircraft was one of a pair of raiders attacking convoys which were intercepted minutes later, near the Bell Rock, by the Hurricane of Squadron Leader Morgan of 43 Squadron. After a chase of around 20 miles, during which the enemy seemed unaware of his presence, Morgan attacked with two three-second bursts, one from 100 yards astern and one from dead ahead at 50 yards, and the Heinkel dived into the sea. Morgan was to suffer engine failure during a fight with a Junkers 88 off Arbroath at 1550 hours on 27 July and, in the subsequent crash, had his front teeth knocked into his palate by the gunsight of his aircraft.

A Junkers 88 crashed at St Cyrus on 14 July 1941, killing the crew of four. At around 0800 hours on 16 August 1941 two 500kg bombs were dropped

Repair Parties get to work following the explosion in Forest Park Place. Local residents had wasted little time in salvaging coal from the Power Station. The roof of Forest Park Cinema can be seen on the left.
FROM THE COLLECTION OF PETER FLETCHER

on the airfield at Arbroath causing no damage or casualties. The following morning two further bombs were dropped on Thomson Terrace in the Rossie Island housing estate, Montrose, and slight damage done to the nearby railway bridge. Fortunately, nobody was killed or seriously injured, although two people were rendered totally deaf by the explosions.

Almost two weeks later, on 1 September, Sergeant Wellings of 43 Squadron was on night patrol practice at 2200 hours when his Hurricane Z2520 crashed into the river west of the Rail Bridge. Wellings was killed in the crash, which took place in clear conditions and for no apparent reason.

The last bomb to be dropped within the city boundary fell 100 yards to the north of Ballochmyle Drive near the junction of Glenconner Drive and Pitkerro Drive at 2000 hours on a clear and moonlit night on 2 November 1941. There were no injuries, although some damage was done to nearby houses. The same aircraft had previously dropped four bombs from approximately 4,000 feet on open ground at Blairfield, Birkhill, and went on to drop another two at Mains of Wellbank. An RAF Defiant on a weather test flight over Fife Ness was ordered to intercept this aircraft, which had been originally plotted as friendly. It was seen to get close by the Royal Observer Corps, but the enemy's rate of climb was too great for the obsolete fighter. A Beaufighter was also scrambled from Drem but was too late to do any good.

At 1210 hours on 2 February 1942 a low-flying aircraft dropped two bombs at Guardbridge, one on the east side of the main road north of the village, and one in the river on the west side of the road, close to the village schools. This aircraft, a Heinkel 111 on a shipping reconnaissance to the Forth and Tay estuaries, had again been plotted as friendly and it was only when it passed, at treetop height, over the Royal Observer Corps post at Guardbridge that it was identified as anything but. One minute later six children and two adults were injured, and Mrs Wilkinson of River Terrace was dead. The village was also strafed during this attack, which left over 40 houses and the paper mill damaged, and the electricity cut. 611 Squadron were scrambled to intercept but failed to make contact with the enemy, who raced off to the north.

One bomb was dropped on the foreshore at Leuchars Airfield on 17 February causing slight injuries to one RAF serviceman.

The worst raid in the area was also the last. It took place on 6 August 1942 after a group of three enemy aircraft had been plotted flying north-west from 100 miles east of Holy Island at 13,000 feet. When they were off Dunbar all three turned west and one aircraft separated from the others to fly up the

Forth. It dropped three bombs in the sea off Prestonpans and one near Portobello, before fading from the plot over Crail where it was picked up by the Royal Observer Corps. At 2335 hours this same aircraft dropped four 500kg bombs on houses at Nelson Street and Park Steet in St Andrews. Seven Beaufighters were scrambled from Drem but no contact was made with any of the three aircraft. The subsequent rescue operations involved parties from Newport, Tayport, Colinsburgh, Cupar, Methil and St Andrews itself. Also on hand were Home Guard pickets, two First Aid Parties, Fire Service, Mortuary and Transport personnel, RAF casualty personnel, gas, water and electricity repair parties, WVS emergency relief workers and a mobile canteen.

The harrowing task that awaited the rescue parties is clearly illustrated by the final situation report at 1730 hours on 8 August. Two families had been wiped out. Seven bodies had been identified of which five were female. Four heads remained unidentifiable and would be buried in a common grave along with other parts of bodies. Apart from the 11 killed, 12 people were injured, six of them seriously. One passer-by had thrown himself over his girlfriend and had been seriously injured by falling masonry. Two houses were demolished in the attack and a further four were beyond repair. Ten houses were rendered uninhabitable and slight damage was done to 20 blocks in the nearby housing scheme.

On the evening of Saturday, 24 April 1943, an aircraft machine gunned the area at the top of the Hilltown and across to Victoria Road. Fortunately, there were no injuries although a number of buildings were damaged by gunfire, including Henderson's Garage on Strathmartine Road and Topping's grocery in Caldrum Street. One rumour circulating on the Hilltown after this incident was that Hitler's only real territorial demand in Europe had always been the Hilltown clock and that perhaps we should just have given him it!

A similar attack took place at 2205 hours on 22 April 1944 when a hostile aircraft flew along the High Street and out over the Harbour towards Broughty Ferry, again strafing. As before there were no casualties. This, the last attack on the Dundee area, took place during celebrations to mark 'Salute the Soldier Week' and, despite bullets ricocheting off the streets, many of those present in City Square thought it was all part of the display!

There were 132 red alerts in Dundee during the war, the first at 1126 hours on Friday, 20 October 1939, being due to enemy aircraft over the Forth. The *People's Journal* reported that the public responded well and without panic to the sirens. A number of women climbing the wall between the tenements in

121

Two Electricity Department officials survey the damage to the Power Station.
FROM THE COLLECTION OF PETER FLETCHER

Scott Street and the trench shelters beside Pentland Avenue were assisted by Corporation workmen, and 150 people made their way to the Law Tunnel. At Downfield, golfers starting the back nine carried on with their game and, in the city centre, cart drivers reluctant to leave their horses had to be ordered to tether them to lamp posts and get to a shelter. The all clear sounded at 1217 hours.

The last alert sounded at 1555 hours on 15 September 1944, the final all clear being signalled at 1648 hours.

A total of 38 bombs fell within the then Dundee city boundary and 194 in the county of Angus, of which 16 failed to explode. One parachute mine fell in Angus, also failing to explode. Perth and Kinross took 196 bombs and Fife 327. By April 1943 the City of Aberdeen had suffered 346 casualties, including 91 people killed, as a result of 216 bombs.

These statistics take no account of the various missiles which came down in the Tay, one of which led to the fourth and final civilian death due to war injuries in the city. Early on the morning of Monday, 5 May 1941, 24-year-old Constable Robert Stirrat was on his beat in Broughty Ferry when he came across a mine which had been washed up on the beach near the junction of Dundas Street and Fisher Street. As he attempted to secure the mine to stop it drifting out to sea, it detonated. Robert Stirrat died that afternoon in Dundee Royal Infirmary.

Chapter Six

'Arm Yourselves, and Be Ye Men of Valour'

(BROADCAST OF 19 MAY 1940, WINSTON CHURCHILL)

During the last days of peace, in August 1939, Dundonians looking out over the river would have been reassured by the sight of the depot ship of the Second Submarine Flotilla, HMS *Forth*, and her charges which included HM Submarines *Porpoise, Swordfish, Seawolf, Cachalot, Oswald, Seahorse, Sterlet, Starfish* and *Triumph*. At Tayport the Sunderland and Singapore flying boats of 210 Squadron Coastal Command lay at their moorings.

At 1100 hours on 28 August 1939 the elderly 'O' class submarine HMS/M *Oxley* secured alongside HMS *Forth* at the Eastern Wharf. She sailed on her first war patrol at 2000 hours on Monday, 4 September, and, in company with HMS/M *Triton* and three other submarines, commenced anti-shipping reconnaissance off the Norwegian coast. At 2030 hours on Sunday, 10 September, *Oxley* surfaced near Obrestad Light, south of Stavanger, and began charging her batteries. Thirty minutes later she became the first naval casualty of the war and the first of seven Dundee-based submarines which would be lost during the Second World War.

Some hours earlier, *Oxley* had been in contact with *Triton* when they had exchanged estimated positions. In *Oxley*'s case this was over seven miles in error, meaning that, when *Triton* sighted a submarine at 2055 hours, reference to *Oxley*'s earlier stated position, speed and course meant that it could not have been her. *Triton*'s commander, Lieutenant Commander Pat Steel, ordered the recognition signal to be flashed at the other submarine but this received no response despite being sent three times. Steel then ordered the firing of a flare which again brought no response and, 15 seconds later, he fired two torpedoes, one of which hit *Oxley* amidships, breaking her in two.

At the subsequent enquiry it was revealed that, not only was *Oxley*'s estimated position wrong, placing her well over four miles inside *Triton*'s patrol sector, but also that the beams of two lighthouses on the Norwegian coast which were visible to *Oxley*'s commander should have told him of this error when he surfaced. It also became clear that the lookouts in *Oxley* had been slack and had not seen the other submarine until it was too late. No blame was attached to *Triton* or her commander.

Of the 54 crew in *Oxley* only her commander, Lieutenant Commander Harold Bowerman, who had just arrived on the conning tower when the torpedo struck, and an able seaman watchkeeper survived to be picked up by the shocked crew of *Triton*.

Though Dundee's potential as a base for submarines had been proven in the First World War, HMS *Forth* left Dundee amid great secrecy at 0215 hours on 14 October 1939 as it was felt that she was not well enough defended in the Tay. So great was the secrecy and haste that many of the crew had to be rounded up from dance halls and cinemas in the city. Ironically, *Forth* sailed almost exactly an hour after the U47 had sunk the old battleship HMS *Royal Oak* inside the Navy's northern stronghold, Scapa Flow, with the loss of 833 lives.

While *Forth* went to Rosyth and from there to the Clyde, many of the submarines began operating from Blyth in Northumberland until proper shore facilities could be provided at Dundee. During this period three more vessels were lost: *Seahorse* was depth charged off the mouth of the Elbe on the afternoon of 7 January 1940 and lost with all hands, *Starfish* was depth charged to the surface in the Heligoland Bight on 20 January, her crew being taken prisoner, and *Sterlet* was lost with her crew of 41 when she was depth charged in the Skagerrak on 18 April.

On the same day that *Sterlet* was sunk, HMS *Ambrose*, the new shore establishment in Dundee and headquarters of the 9th Submarine Flotilla, was formally commissioned. It comprised Carolina House Orphanage, Maryfield Hostel and the former Lindsay and Low jam factory in the Harbour which was turned into a torpedo workshop, NAAFI and accommodation block.

Amongst the first submarines to visit the new base was the French *Achilles* which secured alongside the Eastern Wharf at 1920 hours on 28 April. She was part of a flotilla of ten French boats, along with the depot ship *Jules Verne*, brought north to take part in the Norwegian campaign.

The exploits of the 9th Submarine Flotilla were shrouded in secrecy throughout the war and to this day remain largely unrecorded. Incidents from the operational histories of a small number of the Dundee-based boats do however provide a picture of their little-known and much-underrated work between 1940 and 1945.

General Sikorski and Count Raczynski, the Polish Ambassador, leaving HMS Unicorn *after inspecting the crews of the Polish submarines* Orzel *and* Wilk *in November 1939.*

DUNDEE COURIER AND EVENING TELEGRAPH

HMS/M *Thames*

At 0805 hours on Monday, 22 July 1940, the large River class minelaying submarine HMS *Thames* (Lieutenant Commander W. D. Dunkerley) left her berth at the Eastern Wharf, passing the Bell Rock at 1000 hours. She had just completed a long refit and had orders to patrol off the entrance to the Skagerrak until 4 August.

On Friday, 26 July, *Thames* sighted a German battle group including the battle cruiser *Gniesenau*, the cruiser *Nurnberg* and their screen of destroyers and torpedo boats. At about 1550 hours one of those torpedo boats, the *Luchs,* was approximately 900 yards off *Griesenau*'s port beam when a torpedo track was sighted coming towards her port side. The *Luchs* commander, Lieutenant Commander Kassbaum, tried to take evasive action but before he could do so the torpedo struck, ripping her apart. An hour later only 50 men out of the ship's complement of 155 were picked up alive. It would seem that Dunkerley was concentrating on attacking *Gniesenau* and did not notice *Luchs* cutting across his firing track at 25 knots around 50 yards from his starboard side. The torpedo struck *Luchs* amidships, causing her boilers to explode along with torpedoes in tubes on her deck.

At the time of this attack, *Gniesenau* was returning to Germany for repairs. Included in the damage she had sustained during the campaign in Norway was a torpedo hit from *Thames*'s sister ship HMS/M *Clyde*, also a Dundee boat.

Thames and her crew of 62 never returned to Dundee. From the available evidence it appears that either she was damaged in the explosion which sank the *Luchs,* or she struck a mine while crossing a German-laid minefield 150 miles east of Montrose. There can be no doubt that the attack on the *Gniesenau*, which the unfortunate *Luchs* intercepted, was carried out by the *Thames* as she was the only allied submarine in the immediate area at the time.

S/M *Rubis* FNFL

An early arrival at the Eastern Wharf was the large French mine-laying submarine *Rubis* which was on a mission from Dundee to lay 32 mines off Trondhiem when the French armistice was signed on 22 June 1940. On their return to Dundee the crew elected, almost without exception, to carry on fighting. Their resolve was put under considerable strain, however, on 3 July when the British Government ordered the sinking of the French Atlantic Fleet at Mers-el-Kebir to prevent it falling into enemy hands. Of the 20,000

Commander of Free French Naval Forces, Admiral Muselier, acknowledges an honour guard of French sailors while leaving Mayfield. He is accompanied by Captain James Roper, Commander of the 9th Submarine Flotilla, and (right) Captain Georges Cabanier of the submarine *Rubis*.

Muselier was the centre of an embarrassing incident on New Years' Day 1941 when he was arrested by MI5 on suspicion of being a traitor. After he had spent some days in jail, it was discovered that the evidence against him had been concocted by two disaffected Royal Navy liaison officers.

He was constantly at loggerheads with De Gaulle and, following two major rows which threatened relations between the British and Free French governments, he was sacked in March 1941.

On 3 July 1940, as the Royal Navy took over French Naval vessels in British ports, Cabanier had received a signal from Vice Admiral Max Horton, the then Flag Officer (Submarines).

To: Commanding Officer French Submarine *Rubis*.

From: Vice Admiral (Submarines), Northways, London.

It is with great regret and pain that I must order some restrictions to be placed on the liberty of you, your officers and ship's company, one and all most gallant men who have done unsurpassed work for the Allied cause in the North Sea. I am sure that you will appreciate that where steps of this kind have been ordered generally, it is necessary and advisable to make no exceptions while the situation as a whole remains so complicated. I say this because I, and all those who have served in *Rubis*, have complete confidence in you and all your personnel.

I trust that these measures will only be brief. My sincerest sympathy is with you at the undeserved blow fate has dealt you and yours in recent days.

Should you wish to communicate with me direct, please do so.

The crew were then faced with the stark choice: should they return to France or carry on the fight under British operational control. The seizure of their ship and the attack by the Royal Navy on units of the French Atlantic Fleet at Mers el Kebir, which resulted in the deaths of 1,297 French sailors, caused some hesitation. The decision was soon made, however, and, as Cabanier wrote later, the crew informed him that, "C'est vous qui décidez, nous suivrons où vous irez."

After the war Georges Cabanier became Chef d'état-major de la Marine, Commander in Chief of the French Navy.

Meanwhile, Captain James Roper left Dundee in 1942 and joined the staff of the Flag Officer (Submarines).

FORCES NAVAL FRANÇAISES LIBRES

French sailors in Britain at the time, only 400, including the crew of *Rubis*, rallied to De Gaulle's Free French forces, the remainder returning to France.

With commendable tact, Captain J. G. Roper, the commander of the 9th Flotilla, refrained from the heavy-handed methods adopted elsewhere, merely confining the crew of *Rubis* to the base in HMS *Ambrose* for two days at the end of which they were no less determined to continue the fight against Germany.

Referring to the events surrounding the French Armistice, one crew member wrote recently, 'It would perhaps be fair to mention the part played by the population of Dundee (our operational base) who, during the tragic days of June 1940, continued to offer us exceptional hospitality, this being a central factor in our decision to continue the fight from there.'

By early September *Rubis* was back on patrol off Denmark and, on a subsequent mission which left Dundee at the end of October, an agent was dropped on the Norwegian coast.

In the early afternoon of 21 August 1941 *Rubis* was about to lay 18 mines off the entrance to Egersund, Norway when a 3,000-ton German tanker was seen about eight miles to the north. Despite the fact that minelayer submarines were ordered not to go into action until their full complement of mines had been laid, Henri Rousselot, commander of *Rubis*, immediately trained his deck-mounted torpedo tubes on the target and fired. The torpedo stuck half out of the tube with its motor running, giving off large bubbles of air which were fortunately not detected by the enemy.

Later that afternoon *Rubis* was about to lay the rest of her mines when a German supply convoy was sighted. Quickly laying the mines Rousselot took up an attacking position. When he fired two torpedoes at the *Hogland* (4,360T), his boat was only 400 yards from her target and the resulting explosion, which sank the *Hogland*, also severely damaged *Rubis*. A hatch in the hull was blown off its seating, allowing water to pour into the boat, and had to be closed using a block and tackle. The galley door flew off its hinges and missed Gaston Sanz, the cook, by inches. One of the most vulnerable parts of a submarine was the large bank of batteries which supplied the power for running while submerged. Of the 140 batteries in *Rubis* only 14 remained undamaged after the explosion, with the result that not only was the boat seriously disabled but she also began to fill with highly toxic chlorine gas. When, at around 2100 hours, Rousselot felt that it was safe to attempt to surface, the interior of the boat was almost uninhabitable. Without the benefit of electric motors to drive the boat, great difficulty was experienced in getting her to the surface but eventually, by blowing only the bow tanks, Rousselot brought *Rubis* racing to the surface at an angle of around 50 degrees – much to the relief of his crew.

Though surfaced, the crew's troubles were only beginning. Not only were they a mere two miles from enemy-held coastline and quite unable to dive again, but they were also on the wrong side of the German offshore minefield. While the crew were breathing welcome clean air on deck, engineers in gas masks were working below to get the boat under way again. This included emptying the battery wells of acid which had leaked from the cracked cells, passing it in buckets through the conning tower and emptying it into the sea.

A signal was despatched to Admiral Sir Max Horton, Flag Officer Submarines, informing him of *Rubis*'s plight and the Admiralty began to assemble a rescue force outside the minefield. This squadron included the anti-aircraft cruiser HMS *Curacao*, later rammed and sunk by the *Queen Mary*, four

General Charles De Gaulle, accompanied by Admiral Muselier, on board Rubis *at the west wall of Victoria Dock in 1941 during one of his visits to the Dundee base. Nearest to, and facing, the camera are Henri Rousselot, the submarine's captain, and 'Bacchus', her mascot.*
FORCES NAVAL FRANÇAISES LIBRES

131

destroyers, the armed trawlers *Clevella* and *Filey Bay* and the French ocean-going tug *Abielle IV*, with air cover for the operation provided by RAF Blenheims. In addition, Horton signalled the Dundee-based Dutch submarine 0-14, also on patrol off Norway, and instructed her to make the best speed she could for *Rubis*'s last known position. Should *Rubis* be unable to get under way, 0-14 was to embark her crew and confidential books whereupon she was to sink her.

In the event this would not be necessary as, thanks to the skill of her engineers, and despite losing one man overboard, *Rubis* made the highly dangerous crossing of the minefield after 36 hours spent trapped uncomfortably close to enemy territory and joined her escorts at around 2200 hours on 22 August. She finally secured alongside the Eastern Wharf on 25 August.

On the following Sunday, the priest at St Andrew's Cathedral in the Nethergate was surprised to see practically the entire crew of *Rubis* attending morning mass. Each one had kept his promise to thank God if, by some miracle, he got them out of a seemingly impossible jam.

During the war the *Rubis* was responsible for the destruction of 31 enemy ships and laid a total of 683 mines. By the time she left Scotland in 1945, 21 of her crew had married Dundee girls.

In 1957 *Rubis* was deliberately sunk off Toulon where to this day she serves as a target for Sonar Training. Beside her lie the ashes of her first wartime commander, Lieutenant, later Admiral, Georges Cabanier. Henri Rousselot, her commander for the remainder of the war, received more British decorations than any other French serviceman serving with British forces. He was awarded the DSO, the DSC and two bars.

HMS/M *Truculent*

Under the command of Lieutenant Robbie Alexander, *Truculent*, a new 'T' class boat completed only six months previously, sailed from the 9th Flotilla's forward base at Lerwick on Wednesday, 2 June 1943, on an anti-U-boat patrol. While on passage the following day Alexander received a signal from Flag Officer Submarines informing him that a number of U-boats were known to be heading west across his path for the Atlantic convoy routes.

Shortly after surfacing on the morning of 4 June, a U-boat was spotted some distance away, but was lost sight of when the boat was dived. That afternoon however, a clearer sighting of a U-boat was obtained and immediately *Truculent* dived and turned towards the enemy at full speed. Alexander

132

Captain William Keay of Tay Division Royal Naval Reserve with Polish officers.
FRIGATE UNICORN PRESERVATION SOCIETY

took up a firing position between three and four miles from the U-boat and fired a salvo of six torpedoes, at least two of which found their target. Some minutes later *Truculent* surfaced but found nothing remaining of the *U-308* except for a huge patch of oil containing a large quantity of wreckage.

Truculent remained based in Dundee during 1944 and was in the news again in tragic circumstances in January 1950. She was returning to Sheerness in the Thames on the night of 12 January after sea trials, carrying her full complement of 62 officers and men along with 18 dockyard personnel, when she was rammed by the Swedish tanker *Divina*. Altogether 65 men died, many of them having made their escape from the stricken submarine only to be swept out to sea by the strong tide.

To this day, lights placed on posts at each end of a submarine's deck while surface running at night in order to avoid a repetition of this accident are known as *Truculent* lights.

On the bridge of HMS/M Satyr *while under way with (right) her commander Lieutenant Weston and (left) her First Lieutenant or 'Jimmy', Lieutenant Bennett.*
FROM THE COLLECTION OF BILL WALKER

HMS/M *Satyr*

His Majesty's Submarine *Satyr* left her base at Dundee on the morning of Wednesday, 17 May 1944, passing Lerwick before taking up her tenth patrol off the Lofoten Islands on 13 June. U-boats were sighted on that day and early on 15 June though they were out of effective range. Later on the morning of the 15th, however, the *U-987* was sighted on the surface at a range of 4,500 yards and an attack was mounted. After running fast towards his quarry for eight minutes, Lieutenant Weston, *Satyr*'s commanding officer, fired six torpedoes from a range of 3,000 yards. Though two of the torpedoes appeared to have collided prior to hitting the U-boat, two more were on target, breaking the enemy boat in two. Later that morning a fourth

U-boat was sighted which was again out of effective range. After an eventful patrol and a night alongside at Lerwick on the return journey, *Satyr* secured alongside the destroyer HMS *Chesterfield* at the Eastern Wharf on 26 June.

Satyr was sold to the French Navy in 1952 and broken up in 1962. While *Satyr*'s 'Jolly Roger' was one of only 15 in the Royal Navy during the Second World War which could sport the 'U' symbol denoting success against a U-boat, another Dundee boat would be able to claim even greater distinction.

HMS/M *Venturer*

Though *U-771*, commanded by 28-year-old Oberleutnant Helmut Block, would have a central role in a unique double by HMS/M *Venturer*, she would strike the first blow against allied forces based in and around Dundee. On

Alongside the Eastern Wharf, the crew of Satyr *display their 'Jolly Roger', which shows their six surface-vessel 'kills' along with the 'U' denoting their success against the U-987.*
FROM THE COLLECTION OF BILL WALKER

135

2 August 1944 the U-boat and an armed trawler escort were under way on the surface near Bergen when they were attacked by two Mosquitos of 'B' flight, 333 Squadron Royal Norwegian Air Force based at Leuchars. The two aircraft, E/333 piloted by Lieutenant Commander Jorgensen and S/333 in the hands of Lieutenant Eikemoe, a new pilot on his first operational patrol, were subjected to accurate return fire from both the U-boat and her escort during their attack. They did however hit the submarine with cannon fire, and dropped depth charges from 50 feet which exploded close to the target. Sadly, Lieutenant Eikemoe failed to gain enough height after his attack and struck the mast of the escort vessel. His aircraft crashed into the sea and disintegrated.

U-771 reached Bergen despite the damage she had sustained and, three months later, on 11 November, was on patrol off the Lofoten Islands. At 0839 hours the crew of HMS/M *Venturer* were preparing to dive their boat when *U-771* appeared out of the morning mist at a range of 3,500 yards. Lieutenant Jimmy Launders, *Venturer*'s commander, immediately turned towards the U-boat and fired four torpedoes from a range of approximately 2,000 yards. Ninety seconds later a loud explosion followed by the sounds of a vessel breaking up were heard. There were no survivors from *U-771*.

During her tenth war patrol in January 1945 *Venturer* attacked convoys twice. In the second attack she sank one escort vessel and claimed a possible hit on a 5,000-ton merchant ship. She was back on patrol in February and on the 9th of that month she scored her unique double. At 0932 hours, while running submerged, faint hydrophone effect (HE) was heard on *Venturer*'s sonar. Although this faded at first it was heard again some 40 minutes later and, using the sonar bearing, the officer of the watch began a careful search through the periscope. Some minutes later he sighted the periscope of *U-864*. Excessively loud HE indicating some sort of mechanical problem made tracking the submerged U-boat relatively easy, and it was established that the enemy boat was zig-zagging about a mean course of 120 degrees. With the U-boat's course alterations taking place every ten minutes it was soon possible to predict her movements and at 1210 hours *Venturer* turned to intercept. At 1212 hours a pattern of four torpedoes was fired on an asdic bearing and just over two minutes later one of them found its target.

Jimmy Launders was the only Royal Navy submarine commander of the Second World War to sink two U-boats, and *Venturer* remains the only submarine ever to have sunk another while both boats were submerged. In addition to the U-boats, *Venturer* was responsible for the destruction of

In November 1939 the Duke of Kent inspected the Polish submarine Wilk, *then undergoing a refit in the East Graving Dock. Following him down the gangway are Commander Krawcyk of the* Wilk *and the Naval Officer in Charge, Dundee, Captain Hurt.*
DUNDEE COURIER AND EVENING TELEGRAPH

six merchant ships and one escort vessel. She also claimed a further two merchant ships and one escort vessel as 'probables'.

Despite being bombed three times by RAF aircraft between Dundee and Lerwick, *Venturer* was still based at Dundee in May 1945, and in 1946 joined the Royal Norwegian Navy as *Utstien*.

S/Ms *Orzel* and *Wilk*

On 25 June 1940 Winston Churchill's Private Secretary, John Colville, wrote, 'I hear from all sides that the Poles have been fighting magnificently in France; they seem to be our most formidable allies.' Stubbornly independent and fiercely courageous, the Poles had a deep-seated desire to exact

During the afternoon of Monday, 10 March 1941, the King and Queen visited Dundee. On arriving at Taybridge Station, the King greeted Lord Provost Garnet Wilson with the words, 'Hello, you're new!' Later they toured the Harbour and the Caledon Yard, and are seen here at Camperdown Dock with skippers of armed minesweeping trawlers. Immediately behind the King is Captain Hurt, Naval Officer in Charge, Dundee, while the ratings in the background are from HMS Ambrose.

retribution from those responsible for the rape of their homeland. Many of the familes of these men who had fought their way across Europe and who played a major part in the defence of Scotland in 1940 would suffer grievously at the hands of the Gestapo as a result. Despite this, after the war the trade unions and Government of a grateful Britain colluded in ensuring that Polish ex-servicemen were kept out of well-paid employment.

When Poland was invaded by German forces in September 1939 the submarines *Wilk* and *Orzel* made their escape through the German-controlled Baltic. When they arrived in Scotland, they were found to be short of fuel and to have made the passage without proper charts. This feat was

At the entrance to HMS Ambrose *in Caledon Street, the King and Queen meet officers of the 9th Submarine Flotilla, including its commander, Captain Roper, standing extreme right. Nearest the camera and talking to the Queen is a Dutch officer, Captain G. Helingman, who has just been awarded the DSO.*

acknowledged by General Sikorski, the leader of the Polish Forces in exile, during an inspection of their crews on HMS *Unicorn* in Dundee at the end of 1939. Both vessels, along with another British-built Polish submarine *Dzik*, later operated with great distinction from Dundee.

In April 1940 *Orzel* sent the signal which alerted the British to the invasion of Norway. Soon after this she sank the German troopship *Rio de Janeiro* off Lillesand. She was lost with all hands while on patrol in the Skagerrak in June 1940.

The Polish submariners' pride in their service is illustrated by the fact that the commanding officer of the *Wilk*, Commander Krawcyk, consistently refused to allow Captain Roper, commander of the 9th Flotilla, to go to sea with him as he felt it would show a lack of confidence in him and his crew. In fact, as Roper wrote in 1941, quite the opposite was true. Sadly, this pride and independence was to play a part in a tragic and avoidable incident in July 1941 when, following a breakdown in discipline amongst his crew, Krawcyk committed suicide.

As Roper reported to the Admiralty, he had been aware of problems amongst the crew of the *Wilk* for some time, but any offers of assistance had been refused on the basis that it was a purely Polish matter. What Roper did not know at the time was that amongst other problems Polish sailors had not been properly paid for almost two years. The efforts of Krawcyk and others, including the First Lieutenant of the *Orzel*, to resolve this situation had come to nothing. Unrest amongst the crew led to one rating being arrested in Forfar and a number of others disobeying orders. By June 1941, against the recommendation of Krawcyk and other officers, the Polish naval authorities had decided to break up the crew of *Wilk* and disperse them amongst other boats and flotillas.

On 19 July Krawcyk was due to leave on the night train for a conference with senior officers in London. At 1500 hours he took a telephone call in his

The Norwegian submarines Ula *(P66) and* Utsira *(P85) leave the Eastern Wharf for the last time in July 1945 on their return to newly liberated Norway.*
DUNDEE COURIER AND EVENING TELEGRAPH

office from London at the end of which, without replacing the receiver, he shot himself. During the subsequent investigation it became clear that Krawcyk had been placed in an impossible position by those above him and, with his boat effectively in a state of mutiny, took what he saw as the only way out. In a handwritten note on the file relating to this incident, A. V. Alexander, the First Lord of the Admiralty, comments that the real cause lay in the autocratic attitude of one Polish Admiral.

Wilk survived an attack by a low-flying Junkers 88 while on passage from Rosyth to Dundee in January 1941 and remained based there until the end of the war.

By the beginning of 1941, the base at the Eastern Wharf had taken on a truly polyglot atmosphere with, in addition to the British, Polish and French contingents, vessels of the Norwegian and Dutch navies. Among these were the Norwegian submarines *Ula, Utsira* and *Uredd*, the last named of which was lost to a mine off Bodo in February 1943. A flotilla of five Dutch submarines and their mother ship, the liner *Colombia*, included two, *0-13* and *0-22*, which were lost. In May 1940, as German troops overran Holland, *0-22* was one of two Dutch submarines which made a courageous dash across a German magnetic minefield to reach a British port. Needless to add, providing support for boats and crews from five different countries was a logistical nightmare.

Despite plagues of rats which would often drop on the shoulders of the unwary, Dundee was a particularly popular base with the sailors as the beer in the NAAFI was sold at duty free prices. A pint of beer cost 4d (2p), or 6d (2½ p) for a 'happy days' which was a pint of beer made up with a bottle of strong ale. For the tense and exhausted crews returning from patrol, the beer bar in the NAAFI was the first port of call. One French crew marched straight off their boat and into the bar carrying a large tin bath which they demanded should be filled with beer. Despite the protests of the staff, this was done, whereupon they sat with their feet in it and drank the contents. On one subject there was no argument; the bar shutters always closed promptly at ten p.m. so that the NAAFI girls could have the last two dances at the Empress Ballroom.

A large number of surface vessels used Dundee Harbour during the war, including destroyers and corvettes employed on convoy protection, four Dutch MTBs, minesweepers and support vessels. A visit by an American aircraft carrier soon brought home the reality of rationing. On being invited

Wednesday, 16 May 1945, 1520hrs, over a week after VE Day, and the U-2326 surrenders at the Eastern Wharf. In the background a 'Fifie' can be seen making its way to the Craig Pier. This U-boat left Dundee the next day and was eventually handed over to the French Navy. It later sank with no survivors in the Bay of Biscay.

DUNDEE COURIER AND EVENING TELEGRAPH

The formalities of surrender complete, the Captain and First Lieutenant of the U-2326 are escorted off HMS Unicorn *by a Dutch officer. The First Lieutenant has just suffered a fate common to visitors to the now preserved frigate* Unicorn; *he has bumped his head on the low beam over the entry port.*

DUNDEE COURIER AND EVENING TELEGRAPH

aboard, base personnel stared wide-eyed at supplies of food and fresh fruit not seen in Dundee for years.

In June 1944 HMS/M *Sunfish* was one of four boats being refitted at Dundee prior to being handed over to the Russian Navy. Following a lengthy working up period during which her Russian crew were trained, she sailed carrying her new crew and a small number of British technical advisers. In a case of mistaken identity that was to prove all too common during the war, she was attacked and sunk by an RAF aircraft while on passage. There were no survivors.

HMS *Ambrose* closed after handling her last submarine, *P-318*, in March 1946.

In the air, offensive operations began on 4 September 1939 when a Hudson of 224 Squadron Coastal Command based at Leuchars was in action with a Dornier 18 over the North Sea. Both aircraft were damaged before making for home.

The other Coastal Command Squadron based at Leuchars, 233, then flying obsolete Avro Ansons, did not have such an auspicious start to the war. On 5 September one of their aircraft attacked, fortunately unsuccessfully, the submarine *Seahorse* at the entrance to the Tay. By January 1940, 233 Squadron was also equipped with the more modern Hudson, and on the 10th of that month one of their number was in combat with a Heinkel 111 over the North Sea. Having run out of ammunition, the Hudson crew attempted to bring down the enemy aircraft by dropping 250lb anti-shipping bombs on it.

It was a Hudson of 224 Squadron that found the German *Altmark* off the Norwegian coast in February 1940. This ship, the former supply vessel to the scuttled pocket battleship *Graf Spee*, was carrying almost 300 British

RNR and RNVR officers in the stern cabin of what was then HMS Cressy. *As the newspaper being read by the officer on the left refers to the Second Front, this was probably taken in the summer of 1944.*

FRIGATE UNICORN PRESERVATION SOCIETY

Rear Admiral Robinson VC and Naval Headquarters staff, Dundee, 1944. HMS Unicorn, *the Naval Reserve drill ship in Dundee, served throughout the war as the headquarters of the Naval Officer in Charge, Dundee. By 1941 the Admiralty had clearly forgotten about their old 'wooden wall' at Dundee when they chose* Unicorn *as the name for a new aircraft carrier. After much confusion the Dundee ship had her name changed, eventually becoming HMS* Cressy, *though not before a number of bemused ratings arrived in Dundee to find that the aircraft carrier they were supposed to be joining had been cunningly disguised as a frigate of the Napoleonic era.*

FRIGATE UNICORN PRESERVATION SOCIETY

merchant seamen taken prisoner by the *Graf Spee* the previous year. Having taken refuge in a Norwegian fjord, *Altmark* was later boarded by seamen from HMS *Cossack*. The released prisoners brought back to Leith included Ernest Spiers of 27 Green Street, Arbroath, an engineer on one of *Graf Spee*'s victims, the *Trevannion*.

The patrolling Hudsons came under increased attack following the successful German invasion of Norway, during which they were involved in spotting for naval bombardments, bombing enemy troop and supply ships and carrying out air raids on Bergen and Hamburg. In June 1940 both squadrons were involved in a running fight with the German battleship *Scharnhorst*, during which a number of aircraft were lost.

As convoy protection and anti-shipping patrols continued through 1940, Leuchars was also accepting frequent visits from fighter aircraft damaged or low on fuel following engagements with enemy aircraft over the Forth/Tay area.

On 4 September 1939 Lockheed 14s of British Airways Ltd began a weekly service from Perth to Stavanger, Oslo, Stockholm and Helsinki. They were joined shortly afterwards by three Swedish-registered Junkers JU 52s operated jointly by Swedish and Norwegian crews. These flights by unarmed aircraft were of major diplomatic and industrial importance and would continue throughout the war.

For a short period in February 1940 the service was operated from Montrose, the runway at Perth having become waterlogged and unsuitable for heavy aircraft. In March 1940 the service was taken over by the newly formed British Overseas Airways Corporation. A few days later, one of their Lockheed 14s was captured by the invading German army at Oslo. The crew managed to escape to Sweden from where they were brought back to Perth in a daring high-speed flight over enemy-held territory. Following a break, due not least to appalling weather during the winter of 1940/41, services to Stockholm restarted from Leuchars in March 1941.

Sweden, as the only neutral country in northern Europe, was of particular importance to the British both for propaganda reasons and because that country was the world's largest supplier of ball-bearings. Whilst the ball-bearings were of considerable use to the Allied war effort, it was equally important that the source of supply should be denied to the Germans. In deference to Sweden's neutrality, it was necessary that the flights should carry at least the appearance of being civil, as RAF aircraft would have been immediately interned on landing.

For the first two years of the service BOAC was forced to operate slow and largely unsuitable aircraft until, on 4 February 1943, a De Havilland Mosquito G-AGFV piloted by Captain Clive Holder took off from Leuchars for Bromma Airport, Stockholm. Stripped of all military equipment, the Mosquito's speed was such that it was able to make the trip in daylight. To fit it for its task, a large freight container was suspended in the bomb bay which could carry 1,600 lb of ball-bearings. This container was taken out on occasion to allow the carriage of passengers, for whom the bomb bay was lined with felt and oxygen provided.

Whilst the speed of the Mosquito usually allowed it to stay clear of the enemy, not all flights were trouble-free. During one flight in G-AGFV, Captain Gilbert Rae was attacked by an enemy fighter and had to crash land at a Swedish Air Force base. On another occasion Captain Rae was carrying a passenger to Leuchars when he was attacked. He went into a power dive from 23,000 feet over the Skagerrak, taking violent evasive action until

146

almost at sea level. His radio operator was so badly thrown about that he needed two weeks to recover from his injuries. The passenger fainted but had recovered on arrival at Leuchars an hour later.

Others were not so lucky; on 25 October 1943 the two crew members and an American passenger in Mosquito G-AGGG were killed in a crash landing at Leuchars after their port engine failed. Captain Rae, his radio operator and another pilot being brought back after a crash in Sweden were killed when they ditched in the sea five miles off Leuchars.

On 15 August 1944 Captain Mike Carroll was returning to Leuchars when he saw what he described as a projectile travelling at incredible speed at around 22,000 feet over the Skagerrak. This was one of the first sightings of the German V2 rocket in flight.

One of the last flights by the Leuchars-based Mosquitos took place on 4 May 1945 when Captain Carroll and radio operator Jock Weir flew to Gothenburg, Sweden, in G-AGKO to bring back a Danish courier with the German reply to Allied surrender terms. The trip went smoothly, and they landed back at Leuchars at 0216 hours the next day, two days before the formal surrender was signed.

As the disastrous campaign in Norway turned into a rout, early on the morning of 25 April 1940, and somewhat to the surprise of the Naval Officer in Charge, a Norwegian Air Force seaplane arrived at Peterhead, having flown from Hardanger Fjord. The pilot reported on German shipping movements he had observed near Varaldsoy and this information was passed on to Scottish Air Operations Headquarters at Donibristle. The crew were later entertained by 602 Squadron who watched their stock of malt whisky disappear at an alarming rate.

One of the early passengers carried by the BOAC Stockholm to Leuchars service was a young Norwegian refugee, Jon Roe. Two years later Roe, by then a member of the Norwegian Air Force, was taking part in flights in the opposite direction which were anything but civil in nature. Another escapee from Norway was a former Norwegian civil airline pilot, Commander Finn Lambrechts, and it was he who realised the potential of a small bay on the south side of the Tay as a base for flying boats manned by hand-picked Norwegian crews. 1477 Flight Royal Norwegian Air Force was formed at Woodhaven on 8 February 1942, and the first of the Catalinas that would become a familiar sight on the Tay in the three years that followed touched down on the 18th. It was christened *Vingtor* after the Norse god of war.

Following a period of training, the first operation to Norway took off on 17 April 1942 with Jon Roe as one of the crew. On the way back the Catalina was attacked by a German seaplane and, in the fight which followed, both aircraft were damaged before turning for home.

Early flights were also carried out using a captured Heinkel 115, although this became too dangerous as it was just as likely to be shot down by British as German forces. It was broken up on the beach at Woodhaven.

In May 1943 1477 Flight was absorbed into a new unit, 333 Squadron, of which 'A' flight continued to operate the Catalinas from Woodhaven and 'B' flight began operations with six Mosquito fighter bombers from Leuchars. The Squadron was given the main task of anti-submarine and convoy patrols along with reconnaissance flights on German shipping off Norway. In common with their counterparts from other occupied countries, these men had a strong desire to hit back at the enemy. One Mosquito, supposedly on a navigation exercise, went straight to Norway and shot down a German Dornier 24 flying boat before returning to Woodhaven.

The first confirmed successful action against a U-boat took place on 17 June 1944 when Catalina D/333 piloted by Lieutenant Carl Krafft found *U-423* commanded by Klaus Hacklander on the surface off the Norwegian coast. It was attacked with gunfire and six depth charges, two of which exploded alongside the hull. Six minutes later the U-boat was seen to sink stern first, leaving 40 of the crew struggling in the sea. Exactly a month later, during a Royal visit by King Haakon, Mosquito L/333 took off from Leuchars at 1536 hours. At 1635 hours Lieutenant Liethe and Pilot Officer Skjelanger sighted a U-boat on the surface near Marstien Light on the Norwegian Coast. They attacked using machine guns, cannons and two depth

A Catalina flying-boat of 333 Squadron.
RAF LEUCHARS

148

Seen from a tender, a torpedo mounted in the under-wing rack of a 333 Squadron Catalina at Woodhaven. A temperamental weapon at the best of times, it took considerable skill on the part of the pilot to ensure that torpedoes ran true after launch.

RAF LEUCHARS

charges. These exploded a few feet to port of the stern of the U-boat which was seen to take on a heavy list with the aft deck under water. Liethe and Skjelanger stayed for ten minutes watching as the submarine turned in tight circles to port before submerging stern first. In fact the *U-863*, a type IX D commanded by Kapitanleutnant Dietrich von der Esch, was only damaged and made it back to Bergen the following day. On another occasion the crew of a Mosquito, hit by enemy fire while attacking a U-boat, kept their crippled aircraft airborne just long enough to place their depth charges on target before crashing into the sea and disintegrating. Another Mosquito pilot recovered his aircraft to Leuchars despite having a number of one inch long pieces of shrapnel in his chest.

At 0007 hours on 18 May 1944, Lieutenant Harald Hartmann was flying Catalina D/333 when two U-Boats were sighted on the surface. Hartmann did not have time to execute his attack in the normal manner from directly ahead of the submarine and had to approach from an angle. This exposed the

149

Catalina to a greater field of fire from the Germans and, during the action in which a probable kill was recorded, cannon fire exploded inside the aircraft, mortally wounding one of the rear gunners, Petty Officer Kyrre Berg Danielsen, a fisherman from north Norway. Hartmann recovered the damaged Catalina to Woodhaven at 0530 hours where, with great skill, he managed to land the aircraft almost on to the beach before it sank.

One potentially embarrassing incident occurred in August 1944. Catalina B/333 was on patrol when a tanker was sighted and attacked with gunfire. Almost immediately it was seen to have come from neutral Sweden and the attack was broken off. Somewhat sheepishly, the crew of the Catalina signalled the ship, asking 'How are you?' With typical Nordic courtesy the reply came back, 'Very well, thank you'!

In addition to normal patrols the squadron had developed another clandestine role; their knowledge of the coastline made them ideal for the ferrying of agents in and out of Norway. Carrying radios, generators, guns and explosives, these agents would be dropped off in dinghies or to fishing boats at a prearranged rendezvous indicated by a message on the BBC Norwegian service. Their job was to report back on the movement of German shipping, which would then be attacked by Mosquitos of either the Leuchars or Banff Strike Wings.

It is highly likely that messages from these agents were being received at a top-secret listening post established by MI8c near Friockheim which also had the role of searching for transmissions by enemy agents in Britain.

One such mission took off from Woodhaven at 1415 hours on 6 December 1944, refuelling at Sullom Voe before landing north of Petsamo at 1930 hours the next day. Here a number of passengers were dropped and picked up. The aircraft was damaged and did not get airborne again until 1210 hours on the 8th, flying east to Grasnya in Russia where it remained for four days while repairs were carried out, finally returning to Woodhaven at 1030 hours on 14 December.

On many of these trips a cargo of medical supplies, food and delicacies was carried. The flight to Petsamo took, amongst other things, urgently needed serum. At Christmas, Catalinas would leave the Tay and fly over Norway towing large Norwegian flags. They would then deliver cargoes to their starving countrymen and women which on one occasion included 58,400 Camel cigarettes, 400 boxes of chewing tobacco and 275 boxes of coffee along with chocolate and newspapers.

The Norwegians are still remembered for the contribution they made to

RAF Tealing, 0700hrs, 20 May 1942, and the Russian TB7 bomber bringing Molotov to Britain arrives. In the background are Hurricanes of 56 OTU.

life in Newport and Wormit, one feature of which was the Christmas tree set up every year by squadron personnel at Wormit Church. At Sandford Hill House, Lady Walker would open her home for days at a time to aircrew in need of a rest, and gave the squadron frequent garden parties.

RAF Woodhaven closed in June 1945 and 333 Squadron left for home, where they are still a part of the NATO's northern defences. They still treasure the shrapnel-holed teapot from Harald Hartmann's Catalina.

At 0700 hours on 20 May 1942 a large Russian aircraft appeared out of the morning mist and landed at the newly opened RAF station at Tealing, north of Dundee. Shortly afterwards a small man dressed in a raincoat and trilby hat climbed down from the aircraft and left by car. Tealing's most important visitor of the war was Vyacheslav Mikhailovich Molotov, Stalin's Foreign Minister and Chairman of the Council of People's Commissars. Having visited the Royal Hotel for breakfast, he boarded a special train at Taybridge Station for London where, on 26 May, he signed the Anglo-Russian Friendship Treaty. It would appear that, despite the impassivity for which he was renowned, Molotov was very much relieved to have arrived safely. He promptly awarded the entire crew of the aircraft the Order of Lenin! He had in fact been expected for over a week but, according to official records, he was delayed by weather. It is more likely that he chose to make a diplomatic late entrance following a wrangle with the British Government over the terms of the treaty.

In Dundee the first sign that something was afoot came with the arrival at Taybridge Station of a shuttered train which sat in platform two with steam up for some days. As the Russian Ambassador, Ivan Maisky, a passenger on the train, wrote, 'the town of Dundee is not a very large one, everybody knows one another there and every kind of news spreads among the inhabitants with unusual speed'. The train had been in Dundee for four days when the Lord Provost, Garnet Wilson, accompanied by the Town Clerk, David Latto, came to visit. They were given tea and biscuits. Maisky realised that security was now well and truly breached and decided to return to London, leaving two officials behind at the Royal Hotel to wait for Molotov. Earlier, on 13 May, Maisky and Sir Alexander Cadogan, Permanent Under Secretary of State at the Foreign Office, had been entertained to dinner in the Officers Mess at Tealing House.

RAF Tealing had opened on 27 March 1942 as the base of 56 Operational Training Unit which had the job of taking partially trained pilots and teaching them tactical skills at the same time as developing basic flying capabilities. It was an airfield built in entirely the wrong place, as it lay in a hollow plagued by fog and was surrounded by hills which meant that night flying training had to be undertaken at the small satellite field at Kinnell.

All OTUs had appalling accident rates and Tealing was no exception, the first pilot being killed in a crash at Cupar within days of the station opening. On 6 June 1942 two pilots were killed, one at Purgavie Farm near Kirriemuir and one near Montrose. Three weeks later an American pupil was killed at Newburgh, and on 2 November two pilots, one an instructor, were killed following a mid-air collision over the neighbouring airfield at Balado Bridge near Kinross. On 28 July 1943, Sergeant Carpenter became the 23rd pilot to die when his Hurricane V7725 crashed after a power dive from 22,000 feet. The aircraft came down at the side of Mains Loan in Caird Park, Dundee, leaving a crater over 20 feet deep and 60 feet wide.

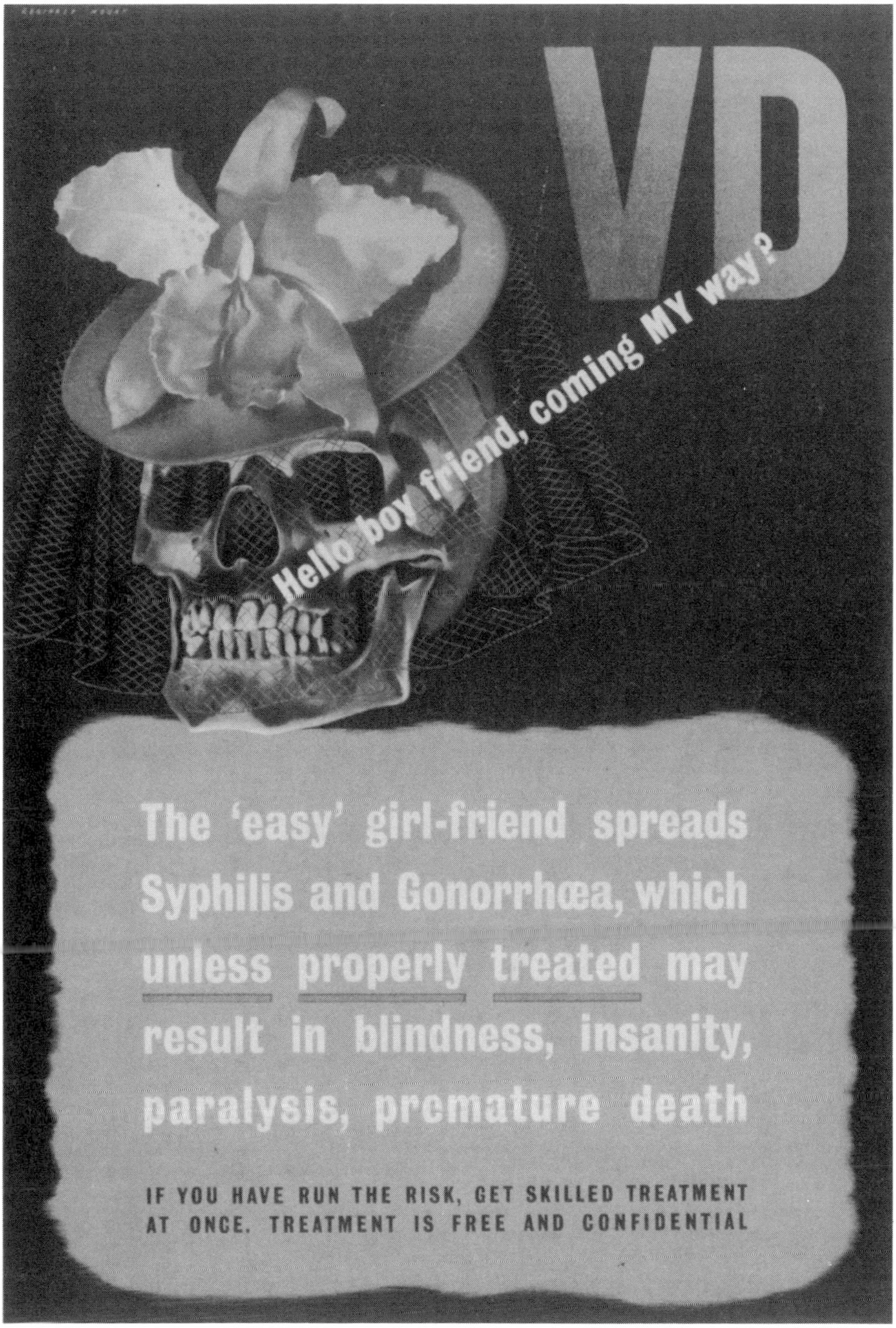
VD
Hello boy friend, coming MY way?
The 'easy' girl-friend spreads Syphilis and Gonorrhœa, which unless properly treated may result in blindness, insanity, paralysis, premature death
IF YOU HAVE RUN THE RISK, GET SKILLED TREATMENT AT ONCE. TREATMENT IS FREE AND CONFIDENTIAL

Others were more fortunate, particularly one sergeant pilot in July 1942 who was acting as the target for another aircraft practising camera gun attacks. The pilot of the attacking aircraft pressed the wrong button and, instead of taking pictures, riddled the target aircraft with machine gun fire. Its pilot, Sergeant Whitehead, bailed out leaving the Hurricane to crash near Arbroath Airfield.

A series of dive bombing exercises held in 1943 was given the strange code name 'Swankpot'. Swankpot 7 involved a practice attack on Bullionfield Paper Works at Invergowrie which was carried out by six Hurricanes escorted by three further squadrons. During Swankpot 15 on 13 June 1943 one Hurricane, flown by Sergeant James, suffered engine failure and crashed into the side of a house in Lochee. Other practice attacks, under the code name 'Roadstead', were carried out on ships in the Tay, the anti-aircraft positions at the north end of the Tay Rail Bridge and on army columns moving between Arbroath and Friockhiem. In one attack on the battle practice target at Lunan Bay an aircraftsman on the ground was shot through the abdomen. Though dangerously ill for some time, he did make a full recovery.

Command of RAF Tealing passed, in March 1943, to Group Captain George Pinkerton, the same officer who had shot down the first German aircraft over Crail on 16 October 1939. By this time improved training and the availability of better aircraft were resulting in fewer accidents, and the more experienced pilots were being used on operational convoy patrols over the North Sea.

That summer the station took part in Operation Tyndall which was designed to deceive the Germans into thinking that an invasion of Norway was about to be launched. Two Horsa gliders were placed conspicuously on the airfield and a large number of tents were erected. Dummy soldiers were even placed at tables in the open air. One officer, viewing a similar dummy camp at RAF Montrose, noted that nobody could really be fooled by this as there were no well-trodden paths between the tents, and the dummy soldiers looked as though they were recovering from what he described as a monumental booze up!

As part of their training, pilots were taught evasion techniques for use should they be shot down over enemy territory. One such exercise involved 13 pilots who were dropped off approximately six miles from the airfield with a compass, map and 6d (2½ p), the object being to return to the airfield without being detected by the Home Guard or the police. The first two pilots were back after two-and-a-half hours having got a lift from the army without speaking a word of English, but the remaining nine were caught. On another occasion, under the code name Operation Grab, the SAS launched a practice attack on the airfield. As this took place on a Saturday evening when most station personnel were enjoying the nightlife of Dundee, Pinkerton had great difficulty in rounding up enough men to defend the airfield. In the event all three SAS saboteurs were, no doubt to their considerable embarrassment, captured by the RAF before they could get to their 'targets'.

RAF Tealing played an active part in the social life of the area, with Dundee Rep and the Blackout Scandals Concert Party entertaining station personnel. Station dances were attended by local people including Lord and Lady Provost Wilson, and various sports tournaments were organised along with the 'Thursday Night at Eight' discussion groups. In September 1943 RAF Tealing chaplains and choir led the Battle of Britain Thanksgiving Service in the Caird Hall.

It appears that some of this social intercourse may have been more active

Early on the morning of Tuesday, 17 October 1939 Airspeed Oxford L9654 of 8 Flying Training School failed to gain height when taking off from RAF Montrose and crashed into the top of Broomfield Signal Box which stood just outside the south-west corner of the airfield. Fortunately, Signalman John Clark was in the cellar filling his coal bucket when the aircraft struck. Nobody was injured and the accident was attributed to the formation of hoar frost on the aircraft's wings.
MONTROSE AERODROME MUSEUM SOCIETY

than the station Medical Officer would have preferred; in January 1944 he noted, with some alarm, a marked increase in the incidence of venereal disease amongst station personnel!

At its peak in late 1943 the unit comprised around 1,500 men and women with 81 Hurricanes, 19 Miles Masters, five Lysanders and three communications aircraft. In September that year over 3,000 hours were flown and 63,181 gallons of fuel used along with 190,105 rounds of .303 ammunition and 1,403 10lb practice bombs. After the invasion of Europe in June 1944 what was by then called No. 1 Tactical Exercise Unit was wound down, although there was a final flurry of activity later that summer when 90 Dakotas were used for a training exercise in emplaning the 52nd Lowland Division. It was planned that this Division would fly into Holland to reinforce the 1st Airborne Division though, perhaps fortunately for them, this was never carried out. Their target was to have been the road bridge over the Rhine at Arnhem, now better known as The Bridge Too Far. RAF Tealing closed on 21 June 1945.

During the war Dundee was once correctly described as 'a city surrounded by airfields'. At RAF Errol Russian crews were being trained on Mosquitos and Albermarles and, in 1944, it became home to the Airspeed Oxfords of 1544 Blind Approach Training Flight. Prior to the invasion of Europe in 1944 Dakota crews were being trained in supply drops at what remains one of the most historic sites in the history of Scottish aviation. It was at Errol that aviation pioneer Preston Watson gave the first demonstrations of powered flight in Scotland during 1906/7.

RAF Whitefield, five miles south west of Coupar Angus, was a satellite field for Perth where 11 Elementary Flying Training School were operating around 90 Tiger Moths, and RAF Stracathro near Brechin opened as a relief landing ground for 8 Service Flying Training School at RAF Montrose in July 1941. At Stravithie, three miles south east of St Andrews, a storage landing ground was opened for 44 Maintenace Unit at RAF Edzell, which held mainly Hurricanes and Wellington bombers.

The naval air station at Arbroath opened as HMS *Condor* in June 1940 and was first used as a Deck Landing Training School. In addition to observer instruction using Swordfish, Albacore and Walrus aircraft, 783 Squadron was formed there as a radar instruction unit. In July 1940 the old First World War seaplane base at Stannergate in Dundee was reopened as HMS *Condor II*. A satellite of Arbroath, it was home to the Walrus flying boats of 751 Detachment and the Vought Kingfishers of 703 Squadron operated on pilot

The Spitfire Mk1 of Flying Officer Brian Carbury of 603 (City of Edinburgh) Squadron, Auxiliary Air Force. It was in this aircraft that he led the section which shot down the Junkers 88 from KG 30 over Montrose at 1400hrs on 3 July 1940. Carbury, a former shoe salesman from New Zealand, would survive the war with 14 victories to his credit. On 10 August 1940 603 Squadron moved south to Hornchurch airfield near London and into the thick of the Battle of Britain.

Remarkably, at least two of the hundreds of fighter aircraft issued to units in the area are known to have survived. After an eventful early career in which it twice crash-landed with battle damage after actions over Dunkirk and during the Battle of Britain, Hurricane Mk1 L1592 was honourably retired to a training role. On 19 February 1943 it was taken on charge by No. 9 Advanced Flying Unit at Errol where it was to remain until 8 October that year. Later it appeared ground-running in the film Angels One Five *before being placed on display in the Science Museum, South Kensington, where it can be seen today.*

Also with a starring role in Angels One Five, *but this time an airworthy one, was the Hurricane Mk1 P2617, a veteran of the Battle of France. From 10 January 1942 until 9 March that year it was attached to No. 8 Flying Training School at Montrose. It now takes pride of place in the RAF Battle of Britain Museum at Hendon.*

MONTROSE AERODROME MUSEUM SOCIETY

Members of F Company of the 1st Battalion, the Highland Regiment, are interviewed by an American war correspondent near Broughty Ferry in May 1942. It is to be hoped that he was suitably impressed by the bayonet secured with string.

training. Overcrowding at Arbroath soon became acute and a further station was opened at East Haven in May 1943. Here, at the quaintly named HMS *Peewit*, the Sea Hurricanes, Swordfishes, Fulmars and Barracudas of 796 Squadron flew on deck landing training.

By 1943, the army had ceased anti-invasion training and was building up its strength for the invasion of Europe which would take place the following year. In Dundee, parties of Commandos and American Rangers were practising street fighting in Blackness Road and the Westport, and the partly built housing scheme at Kirkton became a mock battleground. As part of one exercise held in January 1942, two of the Tay Ferries were used to transport a Polish Mechanised Brigade from Dundee to Newport. In 13 hours 486 vehicles and 2,214 personnel were taken across.

A gunnery school for defensively equipped merchant ships (DEMS) operated in the Harbour and a large WRNS training establishment was set up in Mathers Hotel. Wireless operators for both the Royal and Merchant Navies were being trained at the Dundee Wireless College at 40 Windsor Street.

To the foreign servicemen based in the city the sight of parties of fit, well-trained and well-equipped men on the streets was an indication that their homelands would soon be free. For the Dundonian it meant that the end was in sight and that 12,000 of the city's men and women would soon be home.

During the same demonstration for the press, another member of F Company is about to show the art of 'full kit swimming' in Broughty Ferry harbour. The war diary of the 1st Battalion records that all the correspondents and officers watching were very impressed by the young recruits of this unit, which gave young soldiers of between 18 and 20 intensive military training before posting them on to front-line regiments.

Chapter Seven

'A Happy Reunion'

In December 1941 the Japanese attacked Pearl Harbour and brought America into the war. Though there would be many disasters on the way, survival and eventual victory were now assured. For the Home Front, the war became more a part of everyday existence, and there was a growing sense of resolve to finish the job. In January 1942 the *Courier* suggested the following as New Year resolutions:

Shun complacency.
Hack away all red tape.
Stand up to petty bureaucrats.
Stop snooping.
Fight injustice.
Carry my gas mask.
See the ear plugs aren't lost.
Get someone in the household to learn first aid.
Make sure the whole family knows its job.
Waste no paper.
Learn more about poison gas.
See that the iron rations are ready.
Keep the shelter in good order.
Give the sandbags the once over.
Bank down the fires on the sirens.
Take no chances with the blackout.
Keep the water pails lipping over.
See that the stirrup pump is A1.
Keep my chin up.
Work and work for victory.

In addition, the model citizen of the time never went anywhere without his ration book and identity card, had handed over his binoculars to the Home

Guard and his aluminium pots and pans to make Spitfires, was sparing in his use of the telephone, had the wings of his car painted white to be visible in the blackout and toiled in his garden, obeying the exhortation to dig for victory. It goes without saying that this paragon of virtue, despite the *Courier*'s righteous homily, simply did not exist.

At a time when the bureaucrat reigned supreme it is not hard to imagine the horror with which one Dundee war-widow watched as the youngest of her six children threw her handbag, containing the whole family's ration books, clothing coupons and identity cards, over the side of a Tay Ferry.

It is in any case likely that the *Courier*'s exhortations went largely unheeded that New Year as there was a serious shortage of alcohol in Dundee. Many pubs were reduced to selling lemonade and ginger ale, and consideration was being given to the institution of a 'dry day' on Wednesdays in order to conserve stocks. This must have appeared particularly ironic given the presence of large bonded warehouses in the city which, if the *People's Journal* was to be believed, were crammed with highly volatile spirits ready to explode into a mass of blue flame and incinerate the entire city centre should one bomb land anywhere nearby. By March 1941, such was the level of editorial vitriol being expended in the Thomson press over this issue that Tom Johnston, the newly appointed Secretary of State for Scotland, came to Dundee in order to make peace between the warring factions. His attempt to subdue David Thomson, not surprisingly, came to nothing. On the day of their meeting, having introduced the two men, Garnet Wilson was sent out of the room to wait in the car in Meadowside.

In fact the whisky stored in bonds all over Scotland was being used as much needed foreign exchange to buy arms in America. Some of it was aboard the SS *Politician* when she was wrecked off Eriskay in the Outer Hebrides, the incident which provided the background for Compton Mackenzie's well known tale *Whisky Galore*. The *Politician* herself had previously been known as the *London Merchant* and had worked on the regular run between Dundee and London. As to the whisky, in January 1942 David Thomson was still referring to it in a letter to Garnet Wilson as 'this dangerous menace'.

Early misgivings about women taking up jobs normally undertaken by men had been swept aside in the drive for increased production. With some reluctance, and after much consideration, in 1941 the Corporation agreed to allow women to become 'conductors' on the city's trams though they were never to be allowed to drive them as in other cities. The sight of women working as

Broughty Ferry Scouts pose for a D. C. Thomson photographer outside 32 Monifieth Road while engaged on salvage collection.

From the early days of the war it was realised that morale would be all important and measures to make the public feel a part of the war effort were instituted. Women were encouraged to knit woollen goods for the troops, despite the fact that the wool used was not impregnated against gas – technically making it useless – and schoolchildren made blankets for minesweepers.

Among the great salvage drives which followed was the collection of aluminium pots and pans which were supposedly to be turned into Spitfires. Large piles of discarded cooking utensils grew in Dundee and Perth, despite the fact that, as many were aware, it was quite impossible to make aircraft from them. Many used the salvage collections to get rid of old rubbish and, by mid-August 1940, 789 tons had been collected in Dundee. A collection in one ward is said to have yielded 'a cat's whisker radio set, an ancient talking machine, several cameras, portmanteaux by the dozen and three tons of books'. Another brought forth sewing-machines, wringers and even garden rollers, much of it completely useless junk. Even museum pieces were not immune. A pair of Crimean War guns on display in Dudhope Park were sold for scrap and the £16 raised was given to the WVS.

DUNDEE COURIER AND EVENING TELEGRAPH

brickie's labourers on building an emergency water tank at Constitution Road Bleaching Green in 1942 caused a flurry of comment in the press.

Since 1938 the entire output of the Scottish jute industry had been dedicated to meeting Government contracts and by 1939 Dundee's mills were producing a remarkable 4,500,000 sand bags every week. This was to prove a valuable if short-lived lifeline to an industry which had been staring disaster in the face. By mid-1940, unemployment in the industry was rising again as shipping difficulties and a fall off in the demand for sandbags took their toll and, in 1943, *The Times* was reporting that it was operating at only half capacity.

As the war moved to offence rather than defence, priorities changed to the production of weapons and munitions. Valentine's Perth Road factory had been completing rush orders for gas mask holders, but by 1943 the company was producing ammunition and Ransome and Marles ball-bearings were being fitted to tanks which would take part in the D-Day assuault. Amidst great secrecy, and in collaboration with the University College, the Burndept factory on the Hawkhill was making batteries for the new radio proximity fuse. Earlier, in 1939, the Government Radar Research Establishment had been evacuated to Park Place, Dundee, though it moved again in May 1940 to Swanage in Dorset.

The Caledon Shipyard was at full stretch helping to replace shipping losses, refitting submarines and other naval vessels. The aircraft carrier HMS *Activity* was launched by Lady Gifford during a heavy downpour on Saturday, 30 May 1942, an event which attracted no less than three admirals. Despite a number of strikes during the summer of 1941, which reduced output at a time when it was most needed, 40,000 tons of new ships were launched that year in addition to the repair and conversion work being undertaken.

Jerrycans were being produced in great numbers at Ashton Works. Garnet Wilson writes of one occasion when an urbane director on a time and motion study attempted to offer advice to a girl working there. 'Ugh, away' ya big ***, ah kens ma wark!' came the reply in what he describes as a tearaway Dundee accent.

Partly due to its relative isolation, Dundee missed out on a large amount of war work and unemployment in the city persisted at six per cent as late as August 1941, four times the national average. One result was that many workers were drafted out of the city to factories in England. 1,301 women were drafted in this way, 702 of them volunteered.

Hours in the war-work factories were long and hard, and it was not uncommon to see workers falling sound asleep over their machines. Twelve-hour shifts were common and concert parties were brought in to keep up morale amongst a tired workforce. On the radio every morning there was *Music While You Work*.

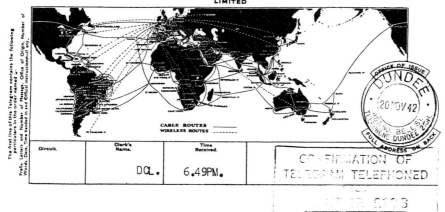

CABLE AND WIRELESS
LIMITED

5/-137

Circuit.	Clerk's Name.	Time Received.
	DCL.	6.49PM.

CONFIRMATION OF
TELEGRAM TELEPHONED

DE379 S CAIRO 20/19 20 1549 BGETAT –   CTF NUMBER OF WORDS

LORD PROVOST OF DUNDEE DUNDEE SCOTLAND –

MA/574 20/11 THANK YOU FOR YOUR ENCOURAGING MESSAGE FROM DUNDEE –

ALEXANDER

MIDEAST .

At 2130hrs on 23 October 1942 the Battle of El Alamein began under a massive artillery barrage. After three years of almost uninterrupted retreat and defeat, the tide of war was, following the entry of America and Russia, at last turning in the Allies' favour.

At Stalingrad that November, the Red Army was launching the attack which would lead to the relief of the city by then under siege for over five months. In 1943, from money raised at an 'Aid to Russia' shop in the High Street, Dundee donated a ward at a Stalingrad hospital.

Amid the widespread euphoria as Montgomery's 8th Army swept across North Africa, his Commander in Chief, General Alexander, received many messages of congratulation, including the one referred to in his reply to Lord Provost Garnet Wilson. It was, as Winston Churchill said on 10 November 1942, 'not the end'. He continued, 'It is not even the beginning of the end. But it is, perhaps, the end of the beginning.' Eighteen months later, as the Allied armada crossed the English Channel on the eve of D-Day, a piper could be heard playing 'Bonnie Dundee'.

FROM THE PAPERS OF SIR GARNET WILSON

Every aspect of life in wartime took on greater intensity and the pursuit of pleasure was no exception. In 1939 there were 27 cinemas in Dundee, and they were to enjoy an unprecedented boom period during the war years. Demand was such that in January 1943 the Caird Hall opened as a cinema with a showing of *Rings on their Fingers* starring Henry Fonda and Gene Tierney. When *Gone with the Wind* opened at Green's Playhouse in 1941 it played for four weeks to packed houses. Given that Green's was the second largest auditorium in Europe at the time, this makes a total of well over 160,000 seats sold, all in a city of 180,000 people. One film not shown in Dundee was an educational item entitled *Birth of a Baby* which the City Magistrates thought likely to deprave the citizens. It was however shown without any fuss to the more pragmatic people of Carnoustie, Laurencekirk and Perth.

At the Kings Theatre in the Cowgate, Garrison Theatre took the stage every Sunday night at seven. Over 300,000 people attended this entertainment for troops stationed in the area between the end of January 1941 and its last performance on 30 September 1945. At the Ice Rink on the Kingsway, Joe Loss and his orchestra were a star attraction. The Palace Theatre in the Nethergate, managed by the prosaically named Leo A. Lion, presented many well known names during the war, including Stephan Grapelli, Jack Radcliffe, Tommy Trinder, Henry Hall and Carroll Levis and his BBC Discoveries. The Repertory Theatre moved to new premises in the Foresters Hall in Nicoll Street where, in 1940, a young Richard Todd was giving 'a fine character study' well down the cast list in *The Constant Nymph*.

In spite of many of their members having been called up, the amateur operatic societies enjoyed renewed popularity. In 1942, Dundee Operatic Society managed to produce *The Gondoliers* by Gilbert and Sullivan 'despite war difficulties' at the Training College Hall in Park Place, and by June 1943 the Blackout Scandals concert party had given over 200 performances. Sunday concerts for charity were a regular feature of wartime Dundee, often being held in cinemas or church halls. Notably, applications for these by groups such as the Daily Worker League were turned down by the Licensing Committee.

For officers, the King George and Queen Elizabeth Club was established at 21 Reform Street, although this became the centre of much disquiet in 1944 when it was found to be refusing membership to non-Home, Dominion or Colonial Officers such as Poles, Norwegians and Dutch. Both Florence Horsburgh, one of the two Dundee MPs, and Lord Provost Garnet Wilson were unsuccessful in their attempts to have this policy changed.

166

By far the most popular entertainment in Dundee for locals and service personnel alike was provided by the city's dance halls. Queues for the Palais in South Tay Street would stretch round into the Nethergate and on a Saturday night every hall would be full to bursting point. This led to real and understandable concern about safety and the placing of limits on capacity, or as it was called at the time, dance hall rationing. Dances were also being held in various other venues, including church halls and the infamous Progress Hall or 'Progie' on the Hilltown where one Dundee soldier was stabbed and killed during a drunken brawl in 1940.

Many a battle royal was fought in the Empress Ballroom between soldiers, sailors and airmen of various nationalities. French sailors, whose favourite weapon was a wine cork placed inside the clenched fist, would unite in hostility with their Dutch, Norwegian, Polish and British counterparts when the Americans arrived on the scene.

This new hedonism outraged more conservative Dundonians and the *Courier* correspondence columns were attracting letters from those bemoaning the fact that Caird Hall concert audiences 'want jazz all the time' and that women of the 'modern set' no longer wore hats in church. One memorable letter complained about some girls who had knocked off the writer's hat and run away giggling, continuing that somebody should 'spank the little hussies'. More than one correspondent condemned 'sabbath breakers' and stated that all war work should cease on Sundays. As late as February 1942 the church itself was condemning the use of Sundays for defence practice. At this time church members were also dismayed to note that young girls were acquiring drinking habits which they termed 'a danger to their health and morals'.

Evidence of wartime shortages in the summer of 1940 had been confined to the almost complete disappearance of advertisements for new cars and the banning, from 5 August, of iced cakes, candied peel and crystallised cherries. At Christmas there were still plenty of goods in the shops including 'Toys for good girls and boys' at Hunter's in the Wellgate. Andrew G. Kidd's were offering a 'delicious, wholesome wartime fig cake' in slabs at 10d (4p) a pound, or traditional black bun at 1/6d (7½p) a pound. Beltona Scottish Records had just released seven new Jimmy Shand recordings at 2/- (10p) each and D. M. Brown's still had doeskin gloves 'for her' at 7/11d (40p). The Ice Rink was holding a 'Grand Hogmanay Gala (fancy dress optional)' which included various races and competitions along with displays by professional pairs skaters Crook and Levitski, and 'Dundee's own Kingsway Ballet', Lena Binnie and Ruby Blake.

By December 1941 there was not much evidence of Christmas cheer despite Andrew G. Kidd's announcement that their cakes were still made with butter. For those wishing to give presents, advertisements in the *Courier* were largely confined to promoting ladies underwear and a 'no coupon bazaar' of practical gifts including soaps, tea, cloths and books at G. L. Wilson's. Soap, soap powder and soap flakes all went on ration from February 1942 and in March the price of a gallon of petrol went up by 1d to 2/1½d (11p). The following month it was announced that, to save material, skirts would be shortened by two inches. By 1943 whisky had become particularly scarce on the open market despite a price rise to 23/- (£1.15) a bottle, but the biggest queues that New Year were for shortbread.

Opportunities for the criminal were greatly increased by the blackout and Dundee, in common with much of the rest of the country, soon found itself in the grip of a crime wave. Reported crime in the city increased by an alarming 35% between 1941 and 1942, with the greater part of the increase coming from housebreakings and theft. Though by 1944 this figure was falling, in January of that year householders in the city were being warned to lock their doors following an epidemic of clock stealing.

The war years also saw a sharp increase in juvenile crime, due in no small measure to the strains placed on family life by husbands being in the forces and wives working long hours in factories. In addition, many wives and dependents of servicemen had been turned into a new class of poor by niggardly subsistence payments from a grateful Government. Wives were given 17/- (85p) per week, plus 5/- (25p) for the first child, 3/- (15p) for the second, 2/- (10p) for the third and 1/- (5p) thereafter. In 1943 Dundee was used as the location for a film on the subject of juvenile delinquency called *Children of the City*. This film of considerable merit provides a graphic picture of social conditions prevalent at the time. Very much a personal statement by its director, Bridget Cooper, it makes an eloquent plea for a more enlightened post-war society.

Before the war almost all Dundee's population was crammed, along with its industry, within a built-up area south of the Kingsway and the Arbroath Road, approximately half the size of today's city. Housing conditions were, even by the standards of the time, simply appalling. A survey in 1935 had revealed chronic overcrowding and deprivation, with 27% of the 47,119 families surveyed living in overcrowded conditions, 2,494 of them living in one-room houses and almost 8,000 in two-room houses. Further, 990 one-room houses were occupied by more than one family and nearly 3,500 houses

DUNDEE SOLDIER'S DREAM OF HOME

Cartoon by Lance Bombardier Robert O. Milne, serving with the Black Watch in France as part of the 51st Highland Division. The regiment fought in North Africa, Sicily, Italy and in Europe following the D-Day invasion in 1944.

On 4 December 1942, 25-year-old Acting Wing Commander Hugh Malcolm of 'Newstead', Albany Road, West Ferry, led a suicidal attack on an enemy airfield in North Africa. His squadron of ten Bisley bombers was not escorted and proved easy prey for the 50 ME 109 fighters which descended on them. None of the Bisleys returned and Malcolm was awarded the Victoria Cross.

BY KIND PERMISSION OF THE MILNE FAMILY

were deemed unfit for human habitation. Among the worst blackspots were Lochee, areas of the Hilltown and the Overgate. Of the Overgate Lord Provost Phin wrote in May 1936, 'The Town Council will be honouring itself by completely clearing out the old properties and substituting modern tenements with the requisite shops and other premises.' Notably, the Town Council was to have been honouring itself rather than the benighted residents of the area. A new policy on housing was drawn up with the aim of building 1,000 new houses every year until 1946 and, although this had hardly got under way when war intervened, the newly completed Beechwood scheme was regarded among the best of its type.

Closely linked to poor housing was the city's poor health record and so as the recession of the Thirties lingered, the health of the city deteriorated. In the year to January 1937 the infant mortality rate in Dundee almost doubled. Outbreaks of influenza and whooping cough contributed to a total of 661 new cases of infectious diseases registered that month, and previously, in May and June 1936, 784 new cases of measles were reported. Throughout the latter half of the decade as many as 160 cases of T.B. were being treated at any one time.

One happier result of the more controlled lifestyle in wartime Dundee was a dramatic improvement in health. Reported cases of mumps dropped from 925 in December 1940 to 324 one year later, and the incidence of measles dropped from 434 in December 1940 to a mere two in the same month the following year. Much of this was due to better health care and to the improved diet imposed by rationing.

While some building did continue into the war years, albeit when civil defence measures should have had greater priority, one of the first signs of post-war planning getting under way came in the summer of 1943 when Dundee's first prefab went on display at Seabraes. In total, Dundee would have 1,550 prefabs at various locations, the first one at 45 Strips of Craigie Road being occupied by repatriated POW Robert McFarlane and his wife. It should be remembered, however, that whilst the primary purpose of prefab housing in other cities, particularly in England, was to replace bombed out homes, in Dundee they provided a quick and easy answer to an existing housing crisis.

By 1942, morale-boosting parades in honour of an important visitor, or as part of a national day of celebration, had become a regular feature of life in wartime Dundee. On Sunday, 15 November that year, which had been designated Civil Defence Day, personnel from all branches of the Police, Civil Defence and Fire Services gathered at Riverside Drive before marching

170

Polish mechanised units opposite Madras College in South Street, St Andrews, during the Warship Week parade in April 1942.

COWIE COLLECTION, UNIVERSITY OF ST ANDREWS LIBRARY

through the city, past the saluting base in City Square, down Whitehall Street and into the Caird Hall by the rear entrance. The Divine Service which followed was a rousing affair beginning with the *Trumpet Voluntary* and ending with *Pomp and Circumstance no. 4* by Elgar. The New Testament Lesson read by the Lord Provost was particularly appropriate to the occasion. *Matthew ch. 25 vs. 34-46* speaks darkly of those on the left hand of God saying that they 'shall go away into everlasting punishment' and, of those on His right hand it concludes that they will go into 'life eternal'.

Parades also formed a major part of the Banner Weeks which were instituted to encourage savings, helping to raise money for the war effort. 'War Weapons Week' in 1941 raised £3,001,453 but the highest total, £4,160,483, was raised during 'Wings for Victory Week' in 1943. For the start of 'Warships Week' on Saturday, 31 January 1942, a naval aircraft was placed in City Square and a display set up in the Caird Hall. The parade was led by a band from HMS *Cochrane* at Rosyth and included WRNS from the training establishment in Mathers Hotel, contingents of the Black Watch and the Polish Army whose goose step particularly impressed the Naval Officer in Charge, even though it did have the habit of knocking their steel

CIVIL DEFENCE

YOUR FOOD IN
WAR-TIME

PUBLIC INFORMATION
LEAFLET   NO. 4

Read   this   and
keep   it   carefully.
You   may   need   it.

Issued from the Lord Privy Seal's Office July, 1939

In the spring of 1942, and in response to the wastage of large quantities of the previous year's crop of oats, the Scottish Farmers Union were holding what were described as 'porridge parties', including one in Dundee, in an attempt to increase consumption.

Wartime propaganda poster by 'Fougasse' (Cyril Kenneth Bird).

THE CORPORATION OF DUNDEE

CIVIL DEFENCE DAY

A DAY OF NATIONAL PRAISE
AND THANKSGIVING

for the defeat of the German air attacks on this country in 1940/41 and for the work of the Civil Defence Services

Divine Service

IN CAIRD HALL, DUNDEE
SUNDAY, 15TH NOVEMBER 1942
AT 3.15 P.M.

Officiants :

REV. HAROLD ROSS, Moderator of the Presbytery of Dundee (Presiding)

REV. R. M. BOYD SCOTT, M.A. (Address)

REV. HARRY ANDREW, MAJOR R. BROWN, REV. F. DRAKE, B.A.,
REV. NEIL M'LACHLAN, REV. JOHN SINCLAIR, B.D. (Convener)

The LORD PROVOST will read the New Testament Lesson

At the Organ :

Mr JAMES HINCHLIFFE, L.R.A.M., A.R.C.M., City Organist

helmets awry. Some disappointment was noted from a number of the surrounding towns for whose warship weeks the navy was unable to supply a detachment, though notable march pasts did take place at Tayport on 18 April and the following week at Monifieth where the salute was taken by Captain King of HMS *Ambrose*.

A range of exhibitions on subjects as diverse as Tyre Economy and Safety of Life at Sea came to the city, including one entitled 'The BBC in Wartime' which ran for three weeks from Saturday, 2 January 1943, and attracted 38,745 people. Amongst the questions asked of BBC staff there was 'Why do the BBC always refer to Scotland as England?' *Plus ça change!*

Since the early days of the war there had been widespread discontent with the bland and, as one observer put it, 'nauseatingly complacent' nature of BBC programmes caused by strict Government controls placed on its output. One correspondent in the *Courier* suggested that BBC programmes should be 'blown up'.

Amongst the many famous visitors to the city in the war years were Sir Kingsley Wood, the Chancellor of Exchequer, who is remembered as suffering from vertigo during a visit to the aircraft carrier HMS *Activity*, then completing at the Caledon Yard. Clement Attlee, Herbert Morrison and Stafford Cripps spoke at public meetings in the Caird Hall as did the then well known author Bernard Newman, who distinguished himself by telling the audience that women would make 'rotten spies' and that they would be 'better employed as messengers'. Other visitors included Field Marshall Wavell and the Dutch Prime Minister in exile, Jan Gerbrandy, who was taken by submarine from Dundee for a nostalgic look at the coastline of his homeland. Crown Prince Olaf of Norway, General De Gaulle and Prince Bernhardt of Holland all inspected their forces in Dundee, the last named piloting his own Beechcraft into Tealing on 25 June 1942. In January 1943 Tealing also entertained the Chinese Air Attaché, Major Huang Pun Yung, who flew, and was suitably impressed by, a Hurricane. As if to prove that a diplomat's life is not an eternal round of caviare and champagne, in October 1942 a Russian emissary, V.T. Yerofeev, arrived in Dundee on board the trawler *Lord Middleton*. The poor man had taken passage in her all the way from Russia, via Iceland.

One notable absentee from Dundee during the war was its former MP, Winston Churchill, and his relationship with the city provides a diverting sideline to the war. He had lost his Dundee seat to Neddy Scrimgeour in 1922, an event which moved T.E. Lawrence to exclaim, 'What bloody shits these Dundeans (*sic*) must be!' Since then, Churchill had stuck to his vow

Just over six months before his death in an air crash, the Duke of Kent, accompanied by the Regional Commissioner, Lord Rosebery, inspected Civil Defence personnel at Dundee in January 1942. He is seen here at the High School with members of the Women's Auxiliary Police Corps, a wartime reserve service set up to release valuable manpower. A somewhat glum-looking Lord Provost Garnet Wilson can be seen behind the left shoulder of Chief Constable Joseph Neilans.
DUNDEE COURIER AND EVENING TELEGRAPH

never to set foot in the city again and his accession to the Prime Minister-ship on 10 May 1940 was greeted by the D.C. Thomson press with undis-guised dismay. The *Courier* editorial on 11 May 1940 is scathing of his defects and describes him as being 'not a reconciling personality' though, given the gravity of the hour, this could only be described as an advantage. For many months the Thomson papers could only bring themselves to mention him by name with the greatest reluctance, restricting themselves to referring to him as 'the Prime Minister'. The first photograph of Churchill did not appear in the *Courier* until January 1941, eight months after he became Prime Minister, and then only as part of an advertisement for the Dundee Savings Bank.

Years before, Churchill had described David Thomson as 'a narrow, bitter, unreasonable being, eaten up with his own conceit, consumed with his own petty arrogance and pursued from day to day, and year to year, by an unrelenting bee in his bonnet'. With the greater economy of words of a journalist, Thomson summed Churchill up as 'a loud-mouthed, bullying, place-seeking show off'.

Matters came to a head when, at a Corporation meeting held on the evening of Thursday, 7 October 1943, the question of whether, in line with tradition, the city should confer its freedom on the Prime Minister was raised. Prior to the debate, the Labour Group had been approached on the matter on a number of occasions and each time had responded with an emphatic 'no'. On this occasion, in a debate where many of the Liberal members were forced to eat their words uttered 20 years before, and where the Socialist Group leader Archie Powrie made the wildly hyperbolic claim that it had been the proudest day of his life when he had thrown Churchill out of Dundee, the motion that the freedom should be conferred was approved by a margin of one vote. One Liberal member is said to have voted the wrong way after being wrongly prompted by his socialist neighbour!

In the event Churchill had the last laugh. He wasted little time in replying and, a mere eight days later, a Corporation meeting is said to have listened in stunned silence as his letter of refusal was read out. All in all an undignified and ill-timed episode.

Although Churchill did not visit Dundee, he did visit St Andrews on Wednesday 23 October 1940, inspecting Polish troops and anti-invasion defences at Tentsmuir, and causing quite a stir on the station when he took time to sign autographs.

From 1943 onwards the minds of politicians and people alike began to turn to post-war planning. The issue of a Tay Road Bridge surfaced again with one suggestion being made that in order to cut costs it could be built on the piers of the old Rail Bridge. Another suggestion made to improve the city's transport links was the construction of a Tay-Clyde canal. Air transport was clearly the coming thing and amidst lengthy discussions about the desirability of having one major airport in central Scotland, the hope was expressed that Leuchars airfield would not be allowed to become derelict after the war.

Following use during the war as a store for the Decontamination (Food) Service and an abortive attempt to turn it into a dog track, football training restarted at Dens Park in 1944. The first game against an Army Select on

5 August ended with Dundee being defeated 7-0. The Civil Defence Services were being wound down and the Home Guard Farewell Parade was held on 3 December 1944, whereupon it was disbanded.

Considerable fears about the effect on the local economy of the return of 12,000 men and women from the armed services and gloomy predictions of a return to pre-war unemployment levels of around 14,000 out of an 'insurable' population of 73,000 were being formulated by the Ministry of Labour. To counter this, a major effort was being made to attract new industry to replace the ailing jute industry, and land was being taken up on either side of the Kingsway for new industrial estates.

Suddenly it was all over. For all too many families there had been the crushing experience of the telegram from the War Office, Air Ministry or the Admiralty intimating the loss of a loved one. For others there had been

Crown Prince, later King, Olaf and senior officers leaving the Norwegian Officers Club at the Caird Rest in the Perth Road, Dundee.
DUNDEE COURIER AND EVENING TELEGRAPH

the long wait, sometimes for over five years, as their husbands or fathers languished in a POW camp. Between September 1941 and the end of the war in Europe, the POW Appeal Fund depot in Yeaman Shore sent 142,000 parcels to Germany. As the first POWs were repatriated in late 1943, Garnet Wilson drafted out a welcome message: 'In the name of your fellow citizens I would welcome you home, home to all the meaning of the precious word. May the passing days bring you health and banish from your mind the evil memories of captivity and that longing for your ain folk which has now been transformed into a happy reunion.'

Somehow appropriately, on VE Day Green's Playhouse was showing a film starring Alan Ladd and Loretta Young entitled *And Now Tomorrow*.

IS YOUR JOURNEY REALLY NECESSARY?

RAILWAY EXECUTIVE COMMITTEE

Chapter Eight

Menace Overcome

Much of the large military machine that existed round Dundee during the war was quickly dismantled after VE Day. Mines had to be lifted from Barry and Monifieth Links, airfields closed and gun batteries dismantled. Some huts lingered into the Fifties and many air raid shelters in 'backies' were still in place until the urban renewal programmes of the Sixties and Seventies.

Of the personalities in wartime Dundee, Garnet Wilson continued as a councillor after giving up the Provost's chair to Archie Powrie in 1946. When he was knighted in 1944 it was pointed out that, while Dundee may have had some hesitation as regards Winston Churchill, there had been none as regards its Lord Provost. He died six months after his second wife in September 1975. Archie Powrie died in harness as Lord Provost in 1949, having been awarded the OBE in 1945. Councillor Willie Hughes became Sapper Hughes W. Royal Engineers in 1943 and, in a letter to Garnet Wilson, described himself in a phrase much in use at the time as 'a filler up of forms'. He too became Lord Provost and, as Lord Hughes, lives in retirement in Perthshire.

Joe Neilans was released from his post as Chief Constable in 1943 to undertake an army staff course, and joined Montgomery's staff in the 21st Army Group. He later worked in civil and military administration in post-war Germany before joining the Ministry of Food in London. He died in Kensington in 1959.

Robert Brown was awarded the BEM in 1943 and made up to Deputy ARP Controller for Scotland. He continued in the police force after the war, retiring with the rank of Superintendent. He died aged 86 in 1987. John Carstairs retired as Deputy Chief Constable in 1947. He became involved in farming and died in 1962. Peter Fletcher was awarded the BEM in 1942. He left the police in 1955 and lives in retirement near Dundee.

To the casual observer little of Dundee's wartime past remains to be seen. Many of the Anderson shelters that caused so much anguish in 1941 still do

Members of the 2nd Battalion, City of Dundee Home Guard, at stand-down in December 1944.
DUNDEE COURIER AND EVENING TELEGRAPH

sterling service as garden sheds, and a concrete surface shelter remains at the side of Arbroath Road in the High School playing fields. At Broughty Castle the firing points for the observed minefield remain, although the site of the Castle Green battery now has the infinitely happier role of children's playground. In the strengthened basement of Coldside Library, the Northern Report and Control Centre still exists in largely its wartime form although without its equipment. At Briarwood Terrace the gap site left after Andrew Moodie's house was bombed on 5 November 1940 remains, and the repairs to the buildings on either side are still visible. In Rosefield Street the tenements which replaced those blown apart that night in November 1940 are clearly discernable.

After the war, serious consideration was given to developing RAF Errol as an airport for Dundee but this was not followed up and it lies derelict, as does RAF Tealing where the runway once used by Molotov's aircraft now provides a base for chicken sheds. The Control Tower and the butts for ranging the guns of the Hurricanes and Mustangs still stand and, at the main entrance to the station beside Kirkton of Tealing church, the remains of the guardhouse can still be seen. At East Haven most of the buildings have gone though three hangars remain in use as farm buildings and the main runway has provided a useful facility for hundreds of learner drivers over the years since 1946. Of the former radar station at RAF Douglas Wood little remains except broken concrete, a number of substantial pillboxes and two air raid shelters in the former WAAF's accommodation site near Downiebank Farm, although part of the site is now used as a training centre for the Scout Movement. One modern communications mast does, however, provide a link with the past. Montrose opened as the first operational air station in the British Isles on 26 February 1913, in fields at Upper Dysart Farm, south of the town. By January 1914, no.2 Squadron, Royal Flying Corps, had moved to what had previously been an army camping ground at Broomfield. Montrose is still an active airfield and three sheds, erected by the Royal Flying Corps in late 1913, still stand as the oldest purpose-built accommodation for military aircraft in Britain, if not the world.

Of the naval base nothing remains although the entrance to HMS *Ambrose* in Caledon Street is almost unchanged and a sign nearby still proclaims the presence of a First Aid and Decontamination Station. The old seaplane shed at RNAS Stannergate was demolished some years ago. Perhaps the site is still haunted by the ghost of one of the officers who served there during the First World War, 'Mad' Major Chris Draper who, on at least one occasion, flew his aircraft through 29 arches of the Rail Bridge in succession.

Many of the coastal defences, such as tank traps, survived the post-war clear up and remain today, notably at Tentsmuir and Carnoustie. Near Alyth there stands an almost complete POW camp used during the war to house captured Italians. Many of the signs above the doors are still legible and two wall paintings in one of the blocks have managed to escape the attentions of the vandals.

August 1945 brought the dropping of atomic bombs on Hiroshima and Nagaski and the end of the war with Japan. On the night of VJ day the City Churches and Broughty Castle were floodlit, as was City Square where revellers danced to the music of the City of Dundee Pipe Band. It was over at last and celebrations continued until the early hours as the city looked with guarded optimism towards the 'broad sunlit uplands' that Winston Churchill

had promised would be the fruits of victory. Sadly, this was to prove illusory, as the end of the war ushered in a new era of austerity and economic decline.

There would be little time for a reckoning before the chill blast of the cold war cut through the warm glow of a costly victory.

VJ Day, 15 August 1945, City Square. At midnight the previous evening the new Prime Minister, Clement Attlee, told the nation that: 'Japan has today surrendered. The last of our enemies is laid low.' He continued, 'Peace has once again come to the world. Let us thank God for this great deliverance and His mercies. Long live the King!'
DUNDEE COURIER AND EVENING TELEGRAPH

Selected Bibliography

Primary Sources

The papers of Sir Garnet Wilson. (By kind permission of the Wilson family).
The Minute Books of Dundee and Tayside Chamber of Commerce.
The papers of Chief Constable Joseph Neilans held by Tayside Police Museum.
The Minutes of Dundee Corporation and its Committees, 1935 to 1945.
The Minute Book of Dundee Fire Guard Service.
Short History of Zone III Home Guard, Col. M.E. Lindsay 1945.
ARP Air Raid Summary, St Andrews District.
Logie School Warden's Post telephone log.
The records of Dundee Harbour ARP Organisation.
Dundee Harbour Trust Wharf Books.
ARP Post Inspection Reports, Dundee.
Military Liaison Committee papers, Dundee.
The Public Record Office, Ruskin Avenue, Kew:
  Various papers in the following categories;
  Admiralty (ADM)
  Air Ministry (AIR)
  Home Office and Ministry of Home Security (HO)
  Ministry of Information (INF)
  War Office (WO)
  Army, Navy and Air Force Lists 1938–1945.
The Scottish Record Office, West Register House, Edinburgh.
  The Minute Book of the High Court, Edinburgh, 1938.
  Various papers filed under HH 50 relating to the Second World War.

Published Works

The Peoples War, Angus Calder. Jonathan Cape 1969.
1940 – Myth and Reality, Clive Ponting. Hamish Hamilton 1990.

The Making of a Lord Provost, Sir Garnet Wilson. David Winter 1966.

Spitfire into War, Air Vice Marshal Sandy Johnson. William Kimber 1986.

Most Secret War, Prof. R. V. Jones. Hamish Hamilton 1978.

Finest Hour – Winston Spencer Churchill 1939 to 1941, Martin Gilbert. William Heinemann 1983.

Operation Sealion, Peter Fleming. First published as *Invasion 1940* by Rupert Hart Davies in 1957.

Stand by to Surface, Richard Baxter. Cassell 1944.

Memoirs of a Soviet Ambassador 1939-1945, Ivan Maisky. Hutchison 1967.

Children of the Benares, Ralph Barker. Methuen 1987.

The Fringes of Power, Sir John Colville. Hodder and Stoughton 1985.

Search, Find and Kill – Coastal Command's U-Boat Successes. Norman L. R. Franks. Aston Publications 1990.

Submarines versus U-boats. Geoffrey Jones. William Kimber 1986.

Battle of Britain Then and Now, ed. Winston Ramsay. After the Battle Publications 1980.

The Blitz Then and Now, vols. I to III, ed. Winston Ramsay. After the Battle Publications 1989.

Action Stations 7, David Smith. Patrick Stephens 1983.

Evacuation in Scotland, Prof. Wm. Boyd. Univ. of London Press 1944.

Winston Churchill – A Seat for Life, Tony Paterson. David Winter 1980.

Hitler's Spies, David Kahn. Hodder and Stoughton 1978.

Beneath the Waves, A History of H.M. Submarine Losses, A. S. Evans. William Kimber & Co 1986.

A Century of the Scottish People 1830–1950, Prof. T. C. Smout. Collins 1986.

Newspaper Files

The Dundee Courier 1937 to 1946.

The People's Journal 1938 to 1946.

The Glasgow Herald 1938.

The Scottish Sunday Express 1955.

The Daily Record 1938.

The Sunday Mail 1938.

The Times 1938 to 1943.

The Perthshire Advertiser 1939 to 1942.

Acknowledgments

Further to the published and archival sources noted above, I must express my incalculable debt to the many institutions and individuals who have tolerated the stream of often obscure requests I have made of them during the 18 months it took to research this story. In this I would include the Local History Department of the Sandeman Library, Perth, and, in particular, the Central Library, Dundee. The staff of the City of Dundee District Council Archives Department, Dundee Museums and Art Galleries, the Registry of Births, Deaths and Marriages in Dundee and the Departments of Printed Books, Photographs and Documents at the Imperial War Museum, London, were all consistently both courteous and helpful. In addition, the Department of Manuscripts, Rare Books and Muniments of St Andrews University Library, along with the Mitchell Library and the Scottish Film Archive in Glasgow, all provided valuable facilities.

Illustrating a venture of this kind relating to Dundee would be quite impossible without access to the files of Messrs. D. C. Thomson & Co. Ltd. I am most grateful to them and, in particular, their Photofile Department for their help so willingly given.

For giving me access to the records of the City of Dundee Police, held in Tayside Police Museum, I owe a considerable debt to the Chief Constable of Tayside Police and especially to Stuart Harris, the museum's curator. These papers were of particular value in helping to unravel the Jessie Jordan story. Also, with regard to Jessie Jordan, I have relied extensively on the recollections of Dr Harry Law Robertson, Mrs Elizabeth Ramsay, whose sister, the late Ella McFarlane, took part in the surveillance operation, and Mrs Ina Reid (née Curran), who kindly gave me access to papers left by her parents.

For his extensive and invaluable memories of both the Jordan affair and the Civil Defence Services I am particularly grateful to ex-Inspector Peter Fletcher who, in his 90th year and despite failing eyesight, read an early draft of Chapter One and made many helpful suggestions.

With regard to the story of the submarine base, I owe much to members of the Submarine Old Comrades Association, including Doug Shepherd, Albert Hamilton (ex HMS/M *Venturer*), Bill Walker (ex HMS/M *Satyr*) and Jean Pierre Babin (ex S/M *Rubis* FNFL). I must also thank Mrs Mary Ireland for her recollections of life in the base as part of the NAAFI staff, and Mme Jaqueline Cabanier for permission to quote from her husband's letter at the start of this book.

For their assistance in building up the story of the war in the air, I would like to thank Ian MacIntosh of Montrose Aerodrome Museum Society, Alex Tough, who gave me valuable insights into the workings of the Royal Observer Corps, and RAF Leuchars Community Relations Office, who helped with the story of 333 Squadron.

This list could, and should, be longer, containing tributes to those such as Group Captain George Pinkerton, Bill Robertson, Charles Lowson, Ron Milne, Alex Cobb, Mrs Jean Rogers and the many others who allowed me to plunder their memories of wartime Dundee. To all of them go my grateful thanks as they do to Mrs Helen Mackersie, who read the proofs and suggested many improvements with commendable patience and tact.